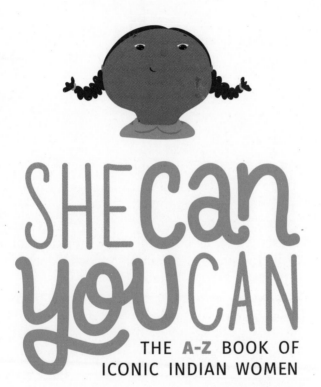

SHE can YOU CAN

THE A-Z BOOK OF ICONIC INDIAN WOMEN

First published in India in 2019 by HarperCollins Children's Books
An imprint of HarperCollins *Publishers*
A-75, Sector 57, Noida, Uttar Pradesh 201301, India
www.harpercollins.co.in

2 4 6 8 10 9 7 5 3 1

P-ISBN: 978-93-5302-564-9

Typeset in Fira Sans Pro 10.74 pt/12

Printed and bound at Replika Press Pvt. Ltd.

HarperCollins*Children'sBooks*

SHE can YOU CAN

THE A-Z BOOK OF ICONIC INDIAN WOMEN

Written by
Garima Kushwaha

Illustrated by
Anastasia Damani

contents

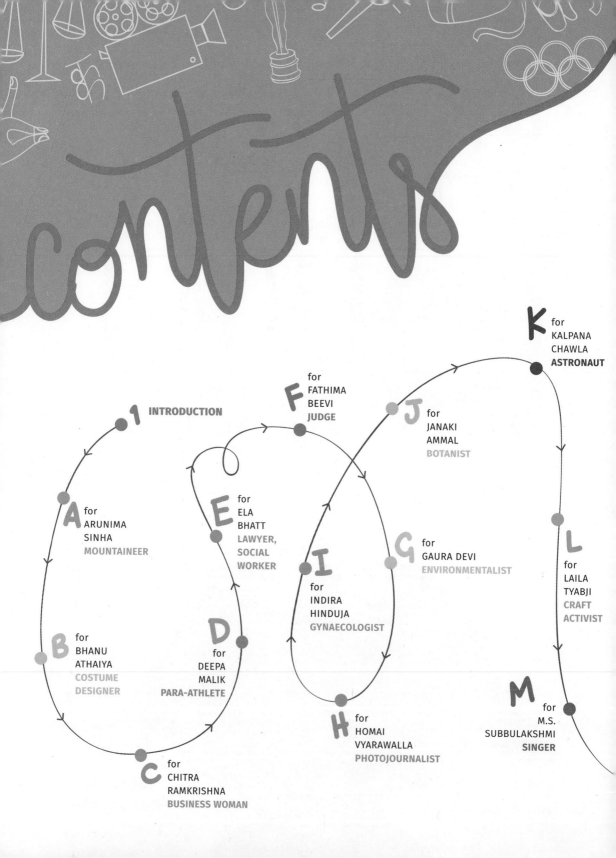

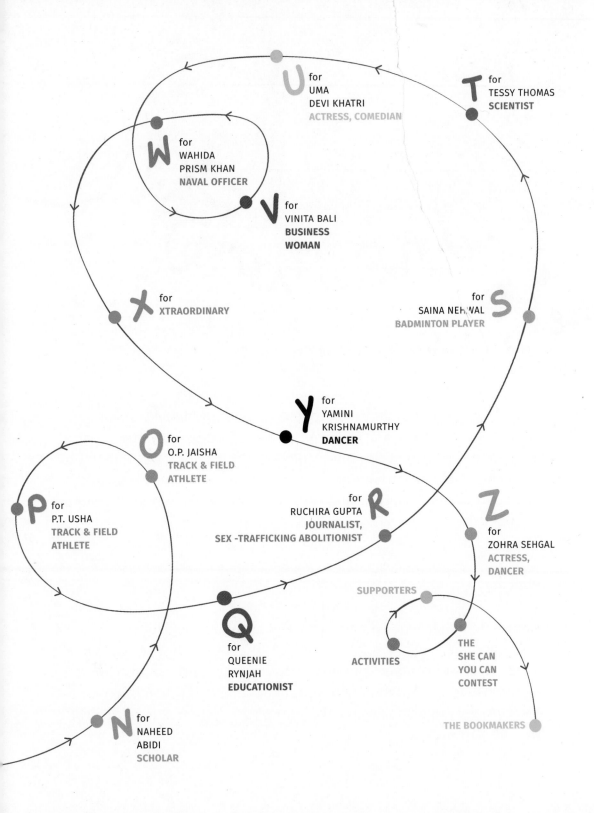

U for
UMA
DEVI KHATRI
ACTRESS, COMEDIAN

T for
TESSY THOMAS **SCIENTIST**

W for
WAHIDA
PRISM KHAN
NAVAL OFFICER

V for
VINITA BALI
**BUSINESS
WOMAN**

X for
XTRAORDINARY

S for
SAINA NEHWAL
BADMINTON PLAYER

Y for
YAMINI
KRISHNAMURTHY
DANCER

O for
O.P. JAISHA
TRACK & FIELD
ATHLETE

P for
P.T. USHA
TRACK & FIELD
ATHLETE

R for
RUCHIRA GUPTA
JOURNALIST,
SEX -TRAFFICKING ABOLITIONIST

Z for
ZOHRA SEHGAL
ACTRESS,
DANCER

SUPPORTERS

Q for
QUEENIE
RYNJAH
EDUCATIONIST

ACTIVITIES

THE
SHE CAN
YOU CAN
CONTEST

N for
NAHEED
ABIDI
SCHOLAR

THE BOOKMAKERS

Introduction

What does the title *She Can You Can* mean?

Hey, you! Yes, you. If you're reading this, you probably already know that India is a patriarchal society, and for a lot of Indian women, life can be like a race stacked against them. Traditionally, there's an assumption that women are not capable of achieving great things – of becoming doctors, astronauts, CEOs or even athletes. Even worse, a large part of our society assumes that women are only suited to work in the kitchen.

With *She Can You Can*, we'd like to stamp this assumption into the mud.

Many bold Indian women have time and again challenged this assumption. Women—yes, ALL women—can do anything they set their minds to. That includes winning against men at sports, piloting robots in outer space, and running billion-dollar companies. Don't believe us? The stories in this book will make you see a different side of the world we call 'patriarchal'.

The point of this book is to feature women who overcame all odds to become legends at what they do. Many of the women mentioned here had it rough. Some had no money. Some were differently abled. Some even had to face armed men all by themselves in a forest. But all of them, through sheer strength of will, prevailed. If they wanted to change the world or make a difference, they did so no matter what came their way.

What does this mean for you? It means that whenever you feel low or feel that life has thrown too much at you, you can take comfort that there have been others who went through difficult times and emerged triumphant. You must have faith that there is the same resilience in you as in these high-achieving role models, which can take you from a difficult place to the summit of success. It also means that men should learn and spread the word about such women and support them in their dreams.

This book catalogues 26 role models. What do we mean by a role model? Why are they necessary?

A role model, simply put, is someone you aspire to become. That doesn't mean that you have to do the exact same thing they did or succeed in the same field. It just means that you look up to them, take inspiration from them and try to align yourself with their path to success. If you are inspired by Saina Nehwal, you would wake up early each morning to practise, just as she did. If Gaura Devi's tale inspires you, you would never back down when it comes to protecting the environment. If Homai Vyarawalla inspires you, you'd know that there is no field out there that a woman cannot excel in.

In our darkest moments, it helps to remember our heroes and our role models. Having someone to look up to gives you the ability to shape your views, ideals and actions. It lets you recognize the kind of person you want to become, and the aspirations and passions that it takes to achieve your life's goals. Role models, more than anything else, are motivators. Every superwoman who tread a certain path made it a little easier for a successor to follow in their footsteps – and go even further beyond.

When we talk about role models from India, most people bring up successful men. Most Indian millennials are unable to name even 10 female role models from their country off the top of their heads. We have grown with our media—internet, books and television—highlighting only the men who are in prominent positions. This is harmful because, as a boy, you could then think of women as not worthy of respect, and as a girl, you wonder if you have the right to be you. For a better world, we need to change this. We need to bring female role models to light so that an entire generation of young Indians, especially its women, can connect and relate to their stories.

Role models like P.T. Usha and Saina Nehwal didn't bring glory to just the women of Kerala and Telangana, nor was their success only for women – it was for the entire nation. Kalpana Chawla died serving no single country or gender, but the scientific aspirations of all of humanity. Gaura Devi, made of steel, fought to protect the forests of her home and ended up starting a movement to protect the forests of the world.

These stories tell us that we must stop seeing gender as a limiting factor, or even as a defining factor. They tell us that not all role models are men and that not all hurdles are insurmountable.

What is this book about? How is it useful?

She Can You Can is an alphabet book that catalogues inspirational Indian women from A to Z. It includes the stories of pioneering female scientists, activists, dancers, comedians and other superwomen from myriad walks of life. The women discussed in this book prove that stereotypical representations of women are irrelevant. By highlighting the brave and fearless accounts of select women's journeys, this book hopes to inspire you on your own journey. Never forget that if **she** can, **you** can!

A
Arunima Sinha
for
awarded the Padma Shri
8848 ft
world's first female amputee & climb mt Everest
"born again on the mountain"

{Arunima Sinha}

'Ghamanja Khilji' – an all-rounder. This was Arunima Sinha's nickname growing up in Ambedkar Nagar, Uttar Pradesh. In a place where young girls were rarely encouraged to take up a sport, Arunima played three – football, hockey and volleyball. She became the primary representative for her school at sporting events and eventually went on to join the national volleyball team.

'It's a moment of pride for the whole nation. The spirit, mental strength and will power of Arunima have been exemplary. She has defied all odds and will be an inspiration for millions throughout the world.'

- Bachendri Pal
The first Indian woman to scale Mount Everest

However, like for many young sportspersons in India, the game alone couldn't pay the bills. To make ends meet, she applied for a job with the Central Industrial Security Force (CISF). Her application was accepted, but a misprint of her name forced her to travel alone to Noida, Uttar Pradesh, to get the error corrected. She boarded the Padmavat Express with a general ticket – a journey that was to change her life forever.

A young woman travelling alone, Arunima was singled out by a group of muggers on the train. They attacked her, assuming it would be an easy

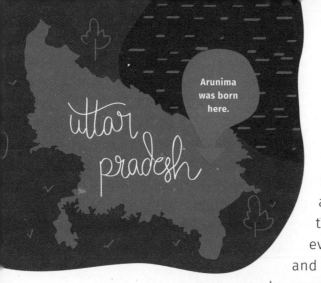

uttar pradesh

Arunima was born here.

robbery. When the young athlete fought back with all her might, the men became more aggressive and managed to force her out of the train. In an unfortunate turn of events, Arunima fell on the tracks, and a train ran over her leg. By the time she was rescued, an entire night had passed. Arunima lost her leg and, in the span of less than 24 hours, lost both her prospects for the job and her career in sports.

Even in the face of such adversities, Arunima persevered. Two years later, she stood atop Mount Everest, her prosthetic leg planted firmly on the highest summit in the world. After the 17-hour ascent, she became the first female amputee to have scaled Everest.

This spectacular feat required intensive training, for which Arunima turned to another superwoman, Bachendri Pal, the first Indian woman to climb Mount Everest. Pal helped Arunima prepare a strict training regime. With her injuries still healing, Arunima toiled endlessly for 18 months. Conquering Mount Everest demanded endurance, mental

6622m Mt CHASER

6189m ISLAND PEAK

8848m Mt EVEREST

1988 — PRESENT

fortitude and, above all, an indomitable spirit. It took Arunima 52 days of acclimatizing and hiking in the Himalayas before she was ready to climb the 8,848-metre (29,029-foot) summit to make history.

With Arunima's limitless resolve, the journey that began on a hospital bed led to a record-setting achievement. She proved that no hardship in life and no physical disability can defeat one's willpower and determination. Arunima told the *Times of India*, 'I chose to climb Mount Everest because it was the toughest thing to do.'

Arunima now wants to help others realize their seemingly impossible goals. She wants to open a free sports academy for the poor and differently abled. Her autobiography, *Born Again on the Mountain: A Story of Losing Everything and Finding It Back*, was released by Prime Minister Narendra Modi in 2014, and through it, she hopes to inspire others to follow their dreams.

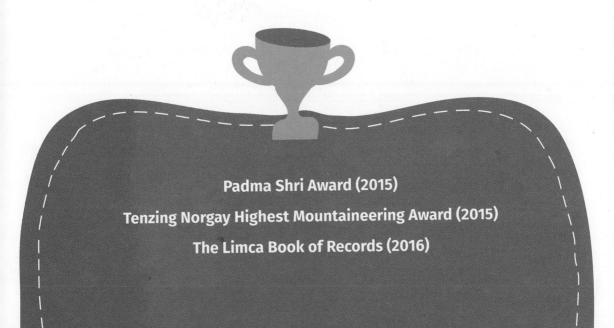

Padma Shri Award (2015)

Tenzing Norgay Highest Mountaineering Award (2015)

The Limca Book of Records (2016)

B for **Bhanu Athaiya**

first Indian to win an Oscar

costume design for over 100 films

Bhanu Athaiya

Bhanu Athaiya fell in love with the creative arts at a very young age. She was born into a family in which everybody studied the sciences. Her father was the first in the family to break the rules by taking up fine arts. Her father's interests gave her several opportunities to explore arts. Growing up, she spent her time painting, watching movies and listening to distinguished guests discuss cinema, photography and art.

'It took me 17 long years to set up *Gandhi, my dream film,* and just 15 minutes to make up my mind that *Bhanu Athaiya* was the right person to create the many hundreds of Indian costumes that would be required to bring it to the screen.'

- Lord Attenborough
Producer of *Gandhi*

At the tender age of 10, Bhanu lost her inspiring father. But this did not stop her journey in the field of arts. She continued to paint with a passion stronger than before, making a place for herself in the field. Her work earned her a gold medal at the prestigious J.J. School of Arts and was exhibited alongside the legendary M.F. Hussain's paintings.

With Bhanu's creativity, however, painting was not enough, and she soon

1929 – PRESENT

shifted her focus to the silver screen with fashion design. She designed dresses for several films and even got opportunities to work with international directors like Richard Attenborough.

Just like her paintings, her fashion design work was exceptional, and at the 55th Oscar Awards ceremony in Los Angeles in 1983, Bhanu Athaiya made history as India's first female Oscar award winner. As light bulbs flashed and crowds rushed in to catch a glimpse of smiling, waving and sashaying stars, Bhanu Athaiya stood tall, clad in a beautiful blue sari. She won the Academy Award for Best Costume Design, along with John Mollo, for designing the costumes for the 1982 biographical epic, *Gandhi*. Designing and styling for a period movie like *Gandhi* and working with some of the best names from Hollywood placed overwhelming pressure on Athaiya. It was her habitual pursuit of excellence that saw her through.

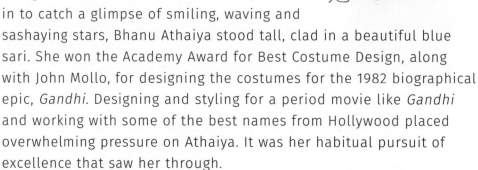

actress Mumtaz's costume

" आज कल तेरे-मेरे प्यार के चर्चे..."

The eponymous movie about Mahatma Gandhi bagged most of the Oscars that year. But the category in which Bhanu won the highest accolade—costume design—was an unappreciated one in her industry. In fact, Bhanu was the first

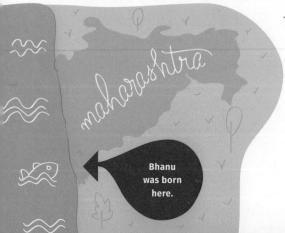

maharashtra

Bhanu was born here.

Academy Award for Best Costume Design (1983)

Nominated for BAFTA Award for Best Costume Design (1983)

National Film Award for Best Costume Design (2002)

credited costume designer in an Indian film. When she went up to receive the golden statuette in front of the crowd at the Dorothy Chandler Pavillion; she began her acceptance speech by saying, 'It's too good to believe.'

At a time when a working woman was a rarity, Bhanu delivered pure artistry through her work. She debuted with *C.I.D.* (1956) and set the fashion stage for classics like *Pyaasa* (1957), *Chaudhvin Ka Chand* (1960) and *Sahib Bibi Aur Ghulam* (1962). She went on to become one of the most revered costume designers in Indian cinema and has worked in over hundred movies since her debut. The most prolific members of the movie business collaborated with her – Guru Dutt, Yash Chopra, Raj Kapoor, Ashutosh Gowariker, and international directors like Conrad Rooks and Richard Attenborough. If a movie required a fine eye for attire—be it a period setting or modern times—she was the one to be called. Most recently, she has worked on *Lagaan* (2001) and *Swades* (2004).

Bhanu's work defined the aesthetic of Indian cinema, giving it the vibrancy and colour that audiences love. Today, a career and portfolio spanning many fruitful decades stand testimony to how much Athaiya loved what she did and how she practised doing it well every single day.

Chitra Ramkrishna

While it is rare to find women in the field of finance, it is even rarer to find them running the stock markets – a field notorious for being dominated by men. Women traders make up less than 15 per cent of the workforce in major investment banks, and even the ones buying the stocks tend to be men. This 'all boys' club started back in the 1830s in Bombay, where India's first stock exchange was launched. It took over a century and one woman to shake things up – Chitra Ramkrishna.

When Chitra was in school, commerce wasn't her first choice of study. She knew very little of the subject but made it her career because she wanted to be financially independent. This choice ended up liberating not only her but also the Indian stock market.

'You not just have to keep pace – you also have to be a little ahead of the curve.'

– Chitra Ramkrishna

In 1992, Chitra Ramkrishna became the only woman to be selected in the team of five that first introduced digital trading to the Indian stock market. The legendary team helped set up and launch the National Stock Exchange (NSE) – a digital, transparent and open-for-all stock exchange that gave the Bombay Stock Exchange (BSE) a run for its

Chitra was born here.

maharashtra

money (quite literally!). The NSE quickly outperformed the BSE to become India's leading stock exchange.

At the NSE, Chitra was instrumental in launching several key initiatives like e-trading, which allowed trading from remote and far-off parts of India. Nearly all the pundits in the Indian broking community opposed Chitra's vision as it was at the height of the Dotcom boom. But Chitra never hesitated to speak her mind or voice her concerns. In a male-dominated field, she stood out because of her leadership and deep knowledge about the market. With her persistence and hard work, Chitra led the Indian stock market into the 21st century.

Besides her achievements in the world of finance, Chitra's childhood fondness for classical music stayed with her throughout her life, and she continued to play the Veena whenever she found the time.

After the NSE was established, Chitra held several positions within

FORTUNE 500

← Chitra was on Fortune's list of 50 most powerful women in business

1963 – PRESENT

the organization, managing its various operational and strategic processes. Due to Chitra's strong leadership skills and her expertise in the stock market, she became the NSE's first female CEO as well as its Managing Director. This was a watershed moment in the field of finance – because of Chitra's many successes, the world began to view women as intelligent and effective leaders.

Visionaries like Chitra showed how shattering the glass ceiling could revolutionize finance for the better. While the wage gap between men and women remains a reality, Chitra demonstrated her financial acumen by earning Rs 44 crore (over 6.4 million dollars) in only three years. Her ambition, vision and career trajectory serve as a reminder for a fast-modernizing India to not take women lightly and to never dismiss their potential.

Forbes India Women Leader of the Year (2013)

One of Fortune's 50 Most Powerful Women in Business (2013)

silver medal winner at Rio Paralympics

D for Deepa malik

motorcyclist

shotputter

swimmer

{Deepa Malik}

At a very young age, Deepa Malik was already a spirited tomboy filled with energy and a great love for adventure. She would climb trees and sneakily borrow her friends' bicycles so she could ride off into the distance. But her entire life came crashing down when she was diagnosed with a tumour in her spinal column.

Despite this setback, Deepa kept a positive outlook. It wasn't long before she was back on bicycles, peddling away into a future with no limits. Her cancer grew, but so did her courage. In 1999, when post-surgical trauma left her paralysed from waist down, Deepa knew she had to be stronger than ever before.

> *'I'm glad it [the paralysis] happened when my husband was away, because I was emotionally distracted. I couldn't afford to give up.'*
>
> *— Deepa Malik*

To keep her home in order, she set up intercoms and walkie-talkies everywhere, so she could oversee her daily chores without depending on other people. Keeping her childhood love of bikes alive and thriving, she became the first differently abled person in the country to receive an official rally licence from the Federation Motor Sports Club of India (FMSCI). She took part in the Raid De Himalayas, the world's highest motorsport event in 2009, and the equally daunting Desert

Storm in 2010. At 17,500 feet, the Raid is a high-stakes off-road race that requires immense skill, concentration and energy. Deepa was, by now, a mother of two and had all of those attributes in spades. The only thing she did not have was her legs. But despite the apparent lack of mobility, she charged through the Raid in an ingeniously modified race vehicle. After eight days of high-stakes racing under sub-zero temperatures, she became the first bilateral leg amputee to clear the event.

To prepare for these arduous bike rides, Deepa also took up swimming. She trained daily, and one day, the Maharashtra Paralympic Sports Association encouraged her to compete in Paralympic events. This sparked off a long and successful career in athletics. Deepa bagged 18 international medals and 15 national ones in several sports. She has made it to the Limca Book of Records

haryana

Deepa
was born
here.

Arjuna Award (2012)

President Role Model Award (2014)

WCRC Leaders Asia Excellence Award (2014)

Silver, Rio Paralympics (2014)

Padma Shri Award (2017)

four times. Most of India learned her name in 2016, when Deepa won a silver medal at the Paralympics. This time, her sport of choice was shot-put, which traditionally begins with the athlete making a strong leg drive and thrusting a heavy metal ball as far into the air as they can. Deepa set records: a personal one for her best throw ever and a national one vas the oldest person in her team.

The more you read about Deepa, the more you'll find that her disability never limited her. She is not only an athlete but also an accomplished swimmer, biker, adventure sports player, entrepreneur, fashionista and a motivational speaker. If it can be done, she has done it!

Deepa Malik serves as an inspiration, encouraging women to break out of comfort zones and pursue their dreams. She is proof that a person's will power and optimism can defy all odds and adversities and that it is possible to emerge victorious in spite of them or even, perhaps, because of them.

1970 — PRESENT

won the Padma bhushan

gandhian

E for ela bhatt

S.E.W.A

self employed women's association

{ Ela Bhatt }

In 1951, in the narrow lanes of a slum near Surat, a shy 18-year-old woman named Ela Bhatt discovered a world wholly alien to her own. It was a time when the newly formed Republic of India was undertaking its first national census, counting its people and their grievances on a street-by-street basis. Ela spent her childhood near the Maynafalia slum, the smell of fish and trash always hanging in the air. It was here that a young man (and Ela's future husband), Ramesh Bhatt, took her through the narrow lanes, where she first saw 'how the other half lived'. And it was through this journey, spent 'wandering through dirty neighbourhoods with a young man whose family one knew nothing about', that Ela found her calling in life.

> *'It is the women who are the leaders in change, and without their participation, poverty can never be removed.'*
>
> *— Ela Bhatt*

Today, Ela is the icon and founder of one of India's most successful cooperative movements – the Self-Employed Women's Association (SEWA). SEWA counts over two million women amongst its ranks. These women, like those who Ela first saw toiling with flowers in their hair in 1951, are part of India's vast and unregulated informal economy, which accounts for nine out of every 10 workers in the country. In 1968, when thousands of workers were laid off from the textile mills, it was their mothers and wives who worked to

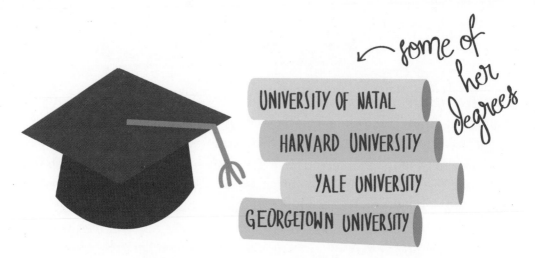

some of
her
degrees

UNIVERSITY OF NATAL

HARVARD UNIVERSITY

YALE UNIVERSITY

GEORGETOWN UNIVERSITY

pay the bills and put food on the table. These women sold fruits, stitched textiles and recycled garbage – all to support their families. Working in the shadow of men, they had the strength to carry entire families on their backs, but they did not have a voice. They did not have a union. And the government did not even consider them to be 'workers'.

Ela realized that this was not simply a 'marginalized' community. They were much more than victims of their circumstances. They were self-employed pillars of society. She founded SEWA as the women's wing of the Textile Mills Association (TLA), based on Mahatma Gandhi's vision of self-sustaining 'village republics'. At the time that SEWA started, most women in the organization were illiterate, with one in three serving as the primary breadwinner for their families.

SEWA means 'service' in Hindi, and what Ela gave these women was the ability to serve themselves – for perhaps the first time in their lives. A union where they negotiated as one, a bank from which they could all withdraw without needing their husband's permission, an insurance policy against

Gujarat

Ela
was born
here.

1933 – PRESENT the worst-case scenario, and the overdue recognition of self-employed working women were some of the services that Ela and SEWA provided to the women of the informal sector. By focusing on women, Ela shone the spotlight on half of India's informal economy.

Ela has also co-founded Women's World Banking, a global network of microfinance organizations that assists women from low socio-economic backgrounds. In addition to her work in economically uplifting women, she has served as a member of the Rajya Sabha, as an adviser to the World Bank and been a member of the NGO called 'The Elders', founded by Nelson Mandela.

Today, at 83, Ela Bhatt continues to battle the stigmas and challenges faced by the working women of India. Thanks to her, Indian women no longer need to work in the shadows and can rely on the full support of a caring cooperative. Her efforts prove that when women empower themselves, the result is an unstoppable force.

Ramon Magsaysay Award for Community Leadership (1977)

Right Livelihood Award (1984)

Padma Shri Award (1985)

Padma Bhushan Award (1986)

Radcliffe Medal (2011)

F for **Fathima Beevi**

won the bharat jyoti award

॥ यतो धर्मस्ततो जय ।

first female judge to be appointed to the Supreme Court of India

first muslim woman appointed to higher judiciary

Fathima Beevi

A country's justice system is reflective of the society that it serves.
To have an unbiased judicial system, people of all genders must be
represented within it. However, it took 39 years for Supreme Court of
India to appoint its first female judge. In 1989, Fathima Beevi overcame
incredible odds and shattered the glass ceiling – an invisible barrier that
keeps women and members of minority groups from moving up in society.
She not only became the first woman judge in the Supreme Court of India
but was also the first Muslim woman to reach this post in all of Asia!

*'The supreme court and the government should appoint
more women in the high courts because the proportion of
lady Judges in high courts is very low. It has to be raised.'*

- Fathima Beevi

Interestingly, Fathima's original plan was to pursue a Master's in
Chemistry, but she switched to law after learning about Anna Chandy,
the first woman judge in India. Anna paved the way for women to take
up law in a country filled with male barristers and judges.

During her time at the Trivandrum Law College, Fathima was one of the
only five female students in her class, and by the time she graduated,

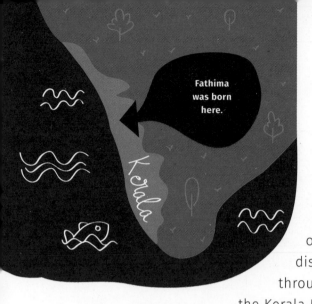

Fathima was born here.

Kerala

that number had dropped to less than three. Persisting with passion, she began her law career in Kerala's lower judiciary and served at several positions within the judicial system over the following three decades. With discipline and perseverance, Beevi rose through the ranks to become a judge at the Kerala High Court in 1983. In 1989, she was appointed as a Supreme Court judge. It was an astounding achievement, given India's starkly patriarchal society at the time.

Beevi's bold and successful career in India's judicial system was not enough to satiate her professional aspirations. After her retirement from the Court in 1992, she served as a member of the National Human Rights Commission and as the Chairman of the Kerala Commission for Backward Classes. In 1997, Fathima was appointed as Governor of Tamil Nadu. As the governor of the state, she made headlines when she rejected the mercy petitions filed by the four sentenced prisoners in the Rajiv Gandhi

She was Governor of the state of Tamil Nadu from 1997 - 2001

Hon. D Litt (1990)

Mahila Shiromani Award (1990)

assassination case. However, later, she was accused of behaving like an agent of the ruling party and failing to uphold the Constitution. This controversy led her to resign in 2001.

By attaining judicial and political positions of such eminence, Fathima Beevi has become a crucial figure in Indian history, her life serving as a guiding light for women everywhere. Beevi showed the world that women are as capable as men in matters of justice and human rights. She proved that if one sets one's mind to it, nothing is unattainable. She demonstrated that career choices for women should not be decided by the diktats of society but by one's own acumen, interests and skills.

1927 – PRESENT

'chipko' activist

G for

Gaura Devi

chairman of over 30 women's groups

मादु हमरु,
पाणि हमरु,
हमरा ही छन सि बौण बी।

पित्रुन लयैं बौण,
हमुनीइ त बचौण बी।

Gaura Devi

Gaura Devi was eight years old when, once, while collecting twigs from the forest with her mother, she asked her why they couldn't just cut a big tree instead of gathering small branches every day. Her mother told her, 'The roots of the trees are like hands. They hold the earth to the side of the mountain. They also hold the water from the big rains and from the melting snow. If anyone ever cuts down our brothers and sisters, our village will be washed away.' This left a deep impact on little Gaura's mind. She vowed to take care of the trees, whom she considered her brothers and sisters, that protected the people of Garhwal and the Himalayan region.

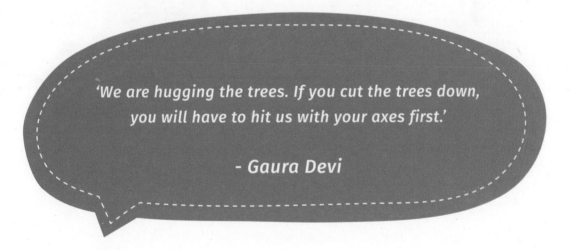

'We are hugging the trees. If you cut the trees down, you will have to hit us with your axes first.'

- Gaura Devi

Years later, she had to defend these values against a ruthless world. On the morning of 26 March 1974, the men of Reni village left for the district town of Chameli to collect their longstanding dues from the government. As they travelled down the road, they passed dozens of labourers and contractors carrying tools, food and, in some cases, weapons. The government had commissioned these workers to cut down 2,471 trees in the forest – trees that were a lifeline for the residents of Reni. The wood was to fetch a pretty penny. The felling of the trees was purposely scheduled on the day the villagers were to leave. As the woodcutters set to work, a little girl saw them in action and ran as fast as she could to the village. The forest meant everything to the people of Reni, and the girl knew only one person who had the strength to save their livelihood: 49-year-old Gaura Devi.

In the 1970s, Gaura was a single mother who ploughed the fields and ran a women's self-help group in the village. When she heard that the forest was in danger, she gathered 20 women and children and marched out to confront the contractors. Gaura pleaded with them to spare the forest, but they did not listen. Faced with the threat of violence, she wielded the only weapon she possessed – her life. She and some of the other women from the village wrapped their hands around the trees and dared the men to take their lives if they wanted to take their trees.

The women stood guard all night, and inspired by this, other villagers from Reni and surrounding areas joined the movement too. Collectively, they chased the contractors and workers away and broke the cement bridge leading into the forests. News of this community effort spearheaded by Gaura spread

the 'chipko' movement involved embracing trees to stop felling

Gaura was born here.

Uttarakhand

across the district and then
to the whole country. Their
nonviolent activism inspired
many spontaneous stand-offs
between the local community and
the timber merchants, ultimately compelling
the government to look into the matter. The courts ruled in favour
of the villagers.

1925 — 1991

Gaura was now called the 'Goddess of the Mountains'. Her efforts led to the birth of the Chipko Movement – the first national ecological campaign led by women! Countless forests owe their existence to these brave women, who moved heaven and earth to protect Mother Nature.

The Chipko movement also spurred the setting up of an environment department and the birth of India's first environment ministry. It led to the introduction of a whole new set of environmental laws – the Forest Conservation Act, 1980 and the Environment Protection Act, 1986. New laws to control pollution and protect natural forests were also put in place and talks about restoring community systems of water and forest management began to make the rounds. The movement gained such momentum that the then Prime Minister Indira Gandhi imposed a 15-year ban on tree-cutting activities in the region till the entire forest cover was regained.

Gaura is now a role model for environmentalists all over the world. Despite having grown up without any formal education, she intuitively understood the harm deforestation could bring in the lowlands. She knew what forests meant to her village people, and the significance of environmental sustainability – something that well-educated people are still trying to understand.

Homai Vyarawalla

In the 40 years between 1929 and 1969, there was only one female photographer capturing history in India. Homai Vyarawalla—clad in a khadi sari and carrying the heavy cameras of yesteryears—was India's first female photojournalist. In the tumultuous period of Partition, Independence and the aftermath, Homai was a regular sight at the front lines of history – taking legendary snaps of everyone from Lord Mountbatten to Jawaharlal Nehru and even the Dalai Lama.

'All I want today is for people, especially the young, to see what it was like to live in those days. It was a different kind of world altogether.'

– Homai Vyarawalla

Even as cameras have become cheaper and photography has become accessible in the 21st century, the field remains quite closed off to women. For her time, Homai was a pioneer, capturing and chronicling the most iconic moments of Indian Independence. Her lens captured the rise of the world's largest democracy.

Homai's childhood was spent constantly on the move. She was born in 1913 into a Parsi family of travelling theatre professionals from Gujarat. Wherever her father went with his group, Homai went as well. The experience opened her eyes to the larger world that was India.

Homai was born here.

gujarat

By the time Homai was 13, she was settled in Bombay. There, she found the first love of her life, Maneckshaw Vyarawalla, who would go on to introduce her to the other love of her life – the camera. For she would marry both Maneckshaw and the camera.

Like many great artists, Homai had small beginnings. Her first assignment was to cover a picnic, and initially, her work had to be published under her husband's name, because no one would publish a woman's work. However, Homai didn't care for credits and continued to work towards improving her art. In 1942, she shifted to Delhi, where an emerging independent India was just waiting to be photographed. There, Homai captured iconic and much-celebrated moments, such as the departure of Lord Mountbatten (India's last British Viceroy) from India, the first raising of independent India's flag, the preparations for Mohandas K. Gandhi's funeral cremation, the arrival of the exiled Dalai Lama to India and some

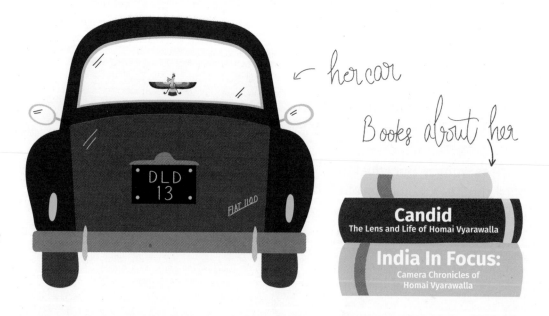

← her car

Books about her

Candid
The Lens and Life of Homai Vyarawalla

India In Focus:
Camera Chronicles of Homai Vyarawalla

of the most well-known candid images of Jawaharlal Nehru.

Homai followed through on her passion and carved out a career in a male-dominated space, in an era when the concept of a working woman was taboo in some senses. A brave and unconventional photographer, she stood out for her ability to capture human emotions, framing them against some of the most pivotal and historic moments of our nation and keeping them alive in our minds forever.

Homai's images can be found in numerous publications, usually under the pseudonym 'Dalda 13'. Vyarawalla considered the number 13 to be a lucky number, as she was born in 1913 and met her future husband at the age of 13. Even her licence plate was DLD 13!

Homai Vyarawalla was a true trailblazer, because she set the precedent for other women to consider a profession that had not been considered a career option before. The image of her riding a bicycle in Delhi's scorching summer and taking pictures—a sole female photographer amongst many men—is revolutionary, to say the least. It tells us something very important: that fearless women can equal men both shoulder to shoulder and lens for lens.

1913 - 2012

won the Padma Shri

delivered one of India's 1st test tube babies

I for indira hinduja

pioneered the gamete intrafallopian transfer

{Indira Hinduja}

March of 2016 was a landmark moment for a girl called Harsha Chavda. Thirty years ago that month, she became one of India's first test-tube babies. Now, in 2016, she was about to give birth to her own child. Expectations were high, because of the longstanding stigma in India about the health and physical development of test-tube babies. But the delivery went flawlessly and a healthy baby boy was born; he weighed 3.18 kg. The magic ingredient during both the deliveries—the one in 1986 and the one 30 years later—was the presence of India's most renowned gynaecologist, Dr Indira Hinduja.

'Over the years, IVF has taken a positive turn with the success rates increasing up to 50%. The purpose of this celebration today is only one, to be reminded and to continually receive encouragement from all the smiles of these children and to follow my pursuit of spreading joy to families.'

– Indira Hinduja

Dr Indira Hinduja pioneered the IVF technology in India and has been a beacon of hope for many childless couples who would otherwise have lived with the heartache of not being able to bear a child of their own. In-Vitro Fertilization would have remained a pipe dream in India had Indira not made it a reality in 1986. As a gynaecologist, obstetrician

Indira grew up here.

maharashtra

and infertility specialist, she has pioneered some of the greatest moments in Indian medical history.

Even though the number of female doctors has risen in India, its extremely rare for a female researcher to make a breakthrough in Indian medicine. Indira is one of the first to have made a mark in the field. She delivered one of the first test-tube babies in India at KEM Hospital in 1986, a result of her three-year-long research in IVF and her relentless pursuit of innovative scientific insights.

Over the years, Indira went on to deliver over 1,500 test-tube babies. Not one to rest easy on her laurels, Indira continued her endeavour in exploring uncharted medical territory. She invented the GIFT technique (Gamete Intra Fallopian Transfer) in 1988, resulting in the

'Harsha' was the first IVF baby Indira delivered

Assisted Reproductive Technologies: Current Methods and Future Directions

birth of India's first GIFT baby and the Oocyte Donation technique (for menopausal women) in 1991.

1946 – PRESENT

Indira introduced these sophisticated medical technologies to India. For thousands of women, particularly those who were unable to conceive in their mid-30s and 40s, Indira's method was the only shot at escaping the social stigma of infertility. By combining basic surgical skills with the know-how of experimental embryology, endocrinology and cell biology, Indira brought forth not only thousands of smiles but also a whole generation that might not have existed without her.

Indira had to learn, research and experiment with multiple strands of medical knowledge in order to pioneer new approaches in stretching the limits of medical know-how. Her courage and ability to take risks and her belief in the life-changing power of scientifically advanced technologies is a source of great inspiration for many girls and boys of the country.

Padma Shri Award (2011)

J for Janaki Ammal

won the padma shri

magnolia kobus janaki ammal

helped create sugarcane hybrids that yields sweeter sugar

first Indian woman to receive a D.Sc. in botany overseas

{Janaki Ammal}

The next time you take a crunchy bite of some delicious Indian sugarcane, remember that it took the paradigm-defying efforts of Padma Shri Dr Janaki Ammal to make it this sweet. When most Indian women could not even make it to high school, this extraordinary woman beat caste and class divisions to become an internationally renowned botanist.

> *'My work is what will survive.'*
>
> *– Janaki Ammal*

Janaki is one of the first Indian women to have received a Doctor of Science (DSc) degree from another country. Janaki studied at the University of Michigan as its first Oriental Barbour Fellow and obtained her honorary DSc to become India's first female botanist with an international doctoral degree.

During the early 1900s, India imported sugar from Papua New Guinea because its own sugar was not sweet enough. Dr Janaki wanted to change this, so she worked with a team of expert scientists at the Sugarcane Breeding Station in Coimbatore to make the perfect cross of sugarcane plants – sweeter and higher yielding. Her efforts paid off, and within five years, Indian sugarcane production doubled and its sweetness

she cross-bred 'janaki brengal' (बैंगन)

janaki established a herbarium of 25,000 plants in jammu

increased! Today, India is the world's second-largest producer of sugar.

Janaki helped analyse the geographical distribution of sugarcane across India and established that the *S. Spontaneum* variety of sugarcane had Indian origins. For her work, the Nobel Laureate Professor C.V. Raman appointed her the Foundation Fellow at the Indian Academy of Sciences. However, her status as a single successful woman did not sit well with her male peers at Coimbatore. Faced with discrimination and sexism, she decided to leave for the United Kingdom, where she then worked with C.D. Darlington to write the monumental *Chromosome Atlas of Cultivated Plants*.

Dr Janaki has a large body of work and is a reputed scientist not just in India but internationally as well. While in England, she conducted chromosome studies over a wide range of garden plants. Magnolia was one of the plants that she worked on and to this day, the Royal Horticultural Society at Wisley has a variety of small white flowers named after her – the 'Magnolia Kobus Janaki Ammal'.

Janaki was born here.

Kerala

Shortly after independence, Dr Janaki was on a flight that included our first Prime Minister Jawaharlal Nehru who personally invited her to return to India in 1951 and reorganize the Botanical Survey of India (BSI). From then onwards, she was employed in the service of the Government of India in various capacities,

1897 – 1984 including as head of the Central Botanical Laboratory in Allahabad.

A pioneering botanist and cytogeneticist, Ammal was also well versed in ecology and biodiversity. She was an ardent environmental activist and thus deeply concerned about the environmental impact of the 'Grow More Food' campaign of the 1940s. She was a crucial figure in the protests held against the building of a hydropower dam across the Kunthipuzha River in Kerala's Silent Valley. She was also invited to the landmark international symposium on environmental history, 'Man's Role in Changing the Face of the Earth', making her the only female invitee amongst a guest list that included the world's most renowned environmentalists.

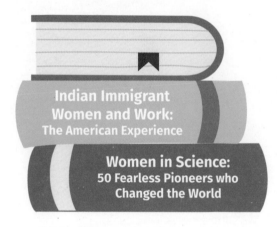

Indian Immigrant Women and Work: The American Experience

Women in Science: 50 Fearless Pioneers who Changed the World

Dr Janaki's many successes in the field of botany make her an incredible role model for any girl.

Elected Fellow of the Indian Academy of Sciences (1935)

Padma Shri Award (1977)

Kalpana Chawla

Growing up in Karnal, Haryana, Kalpana Chawla used to look up at the clear skies speckled with constellations. Often, she would spot a shooting star and wonder what they were. As an adult, she had the privilege of another view – looking down at Earth from the other side of the sky.

> *'I never truly thought of being the first or second someone. Or being a small-town girl. This is just something I wanted to do. It was very important for me to enjoy it. If you want to do something, what does it matter where you are ranked? Nor does being a woman make a difference.'*
>
> *– Kalpana Chawla*

The inhabitants of that small town in Haryana kept their eyes peeled for many years, watching for one of their own who had made the big leap into the cosmos – Kalpana, the first woman of Indian origin to fly into space.

In 1982, after acquiring a Bachelor of Science degree in Aeronautical Engineering from Punjab Engineering College, Kalpana left for the US. There, she earned a Master's degree from the University of Texas and a PhD from the University of Colorado, with a focus on aeronautical engineering. When she got a break with NASA, she joined the Ames Research Centre. Only the brightest and fittest are selected for NASA's

haryana

astronaut programme. She was then selected from an application pool of 2,962 people, as one of 23 astronauts—of which only five were women—chosen to fly in the Space Shuttle.

The Space Shuttle programme was one of the most ambitious endeavours in human history. Carrying a crew of seven to the limits of earth's atmosphere and back, it represented the cutting-edge technology of modern spaceflight. In November 1997, Kalpana went aboard the Space Shuttle Columbia as a mission specialist on flight STS-87, tasked with operating the robotic arm. The shuttle orbited Earth for over two weeks, carrying out several experiments.

Kalpana described her first trip into space to writer Warren E. Leary as 'Alice in Wonderland floating freely, and the Earth moving there below – as if I'd taken the "shrink-me" pill and seen the whole world go by in no time.' So when she got another chance to fly in 2003, she grabbed the opportunity without hesitation. She was selected as the flight engineer and mission specialist for Columbia flight STS-107. When she described on radio the awe-inspiring moment of stars reflecting in her eyes during a moving sunset, you could hear the joy in Kalpana's voice. 'In the retina of my eye, the whole Earth and the sky could be seen reflected,' said Kalpana.

She conducted 80 experiments in space and declared on the radio that her mission was complete. Along with the STS107 mission, Chawla

Kalpana Chawla :
A Life

NASA Distinguished Service Medal (2003)

Congressional Space Medal of Honor (2004)

NASA Space Flight Medal (2004)

KALPANA
CHAWLA WAY

74ᵗʰ street in Jackson Heights, NY has been renamed in her honour

completed her life's final mission. While she strapped herself in the shuttle to return to the Earth's atmosphere, space claimed her life.

Kalpana Chawla made unconventional choices for her time – from opting for aerospace engineering as a young student to becoming an astronaut as a woman. She always said that it was her perseverance and hard work that made her dreams come true. Many places have been named in her honour, but one stands out: the Chawla Hill on the surface of Mars, which bears immortal testimony to this brave astronaut who gave her life for humanity's place amongst the stars.

1962 – 2003

won the padma shri

L for laila
tyabji

crafts activist & social worker

'dastkar'

{ Laila Tyabji }

When Laila Tyabji first landed in Bombay, she felt alien in the country. Having grown up in Belgium, where her father served as an Indian ambassador, she was pale-skinned and spoke only French. In her own words, she felt like a joke in India. But some hurdles are only so at a particular age. Laila, now in her 70s, is a renowned crafts designer who has revolutionized India's traditional handicrafts industry.

'Laila is knowledge-oriented, decisive and endlessly patient without using her personal influence to change the tide of things.'

– Shelly Jain
Personnel and Programme Head at **Dastkar**

'There I was, an urban, westernized, motorcycle-riding girl, thrown into a culture of which I knew little,' said Laila Tyabji recalling the design consultancy assignment in Kutch at the start of her career in 1978. She was assigned to figure out how local craftsmen in Kutch could find new urban markets by the Gujarat State Handloom and Handicrafts Development Corporation. The task at hand was exhilarating for Laila, since crafting products at scale was very new to the Kutchi artisans. It was here that the idea of Dastkar—now an internationally recognized organization—came to Laila Tyabji.

in her 30s Laila used to ride a motorcycle

Tyabji's return from Kutch brought another watershed moment in her life, which she calls 'the incident with the baskets'. She worked as merchandiser for Taj Mansingh hotel in Delhi, where she sold cane baskets from the Assam Emporium. She saw a big demand for these artisan baskets, but the hotel could not justify the cost of the prime real estate that those baskets were occupying for their selling price. Moreover, the Assam Emporium refused to provide the baskets, as it would cost them too much in transportation.

From such events, Laila realized that India is a powerhouse of ancient creativity, but getting small rural artisans to become a sustainable part of the mainstream retail chain is hard. She saw that indigenous art forms were fast losing out to the rise of mills and power looms, even though they were high in quality and looked unique. They lacked the kind of marketing and logistics help that is required to bring products into the streets of urban India – and this is where Laila stepped in.

In 1981, Laila co-founded Dastkar to provide rural craftspeople access to lucrative urban markets. It began with just 15 groups and now works with 350 of them, encompassing everything from textiles and paintings to paper and metal works. By giving rural artisans these opportunities, Laila helped develop self-sustainable craft communities and gave many villages a stable source of income. She

Laila was born here.

delhi

1947 - PRESENT

works with numerous crafts-promoting organizations, such as the Self-Employed Women's Association (SEWA) and other NGOs that promote craft as a means of earning and empowerment.

When she's not bringing ancient Indian crafts into urban markets, Laila is a dedicated scholar. Her works include *Threads and Voices: Behind the Indian Textile Tradition* and numerous articles in Indian journals. Her writing focuses on the inclusion of the crafts industry amongst India's key employment sectors and urges India's economists and planners to treat craftspeople as assets, not liabilities.

Laila is also renowned for making the sari cool again. On her 50th birthday, Laila resolved to switch entirely to saris. She wanted to challenge the notion that wearing a sari makes one look like a 'behenji', someone who is unfashionable or uncool. She led a campaign that focused on the garment's intricate details, from the various draping styles to the distinctive weave from different states that makes each sari unique.

Young women love Laila's fashion sense and her dauntless love for the saris. Simply put, Laila has made the sari cool again. And every day, she helps thousands of traditional crafts sustain themselves, keeping alive an ancient tradition of beauty and aesthetic within the framework of contemporary fashion. For consumers and producers alike, Laila is the bridge that brings us closer to our unique national heritage.

Threads & Voices:
Behind the Indian
Textile Tradition

M.S. Subbulakshmi

As a young child, M.S. Subbulakshmi learnt and practised music with her siblings. Music was a fun activity for the kids. Subbulakshmi's sister, Vadivathe, would play the veena while Saktivel, her brother, would make the room echo with his mridangam. And backing the two with her melodious voice would be Subbulakshmi. But even as they laughed and talked during practice, the three kids kept an ear out for their mother's footsteps, as she didn't like such distractions. Theirs was a highly disciplined home.

> *'M.S. was born to music, she lived as music and finally merged with the god of music.'*
>
> **- A.P.J. Abdul Kalam**
> **Former President of India**

Years later, Subbulakshmi's voice filled the silence in countless homes and souls across India. Trained in Carnatic music, Subbulakshmi performed her first-ever concert at the Madras Music Academy at the tender age of 13. She broke records as one of the youngest musicians at the academy, surprising critics with her spellbinding performance. She joined the ranks of the leading Carnatic vocalists of her time.

When Mahatma Gandhi was in a slump following the Partition of India, only one voice had the power to cheer his spirits. On his request, sari-clad and sitting by his side, M.S. Subbulakshmi sang a paean to Ram. Such was its effect that for the first time after witnessing days of endless violence, the Mahatma smiled. Later that year, on his birthday, he asked

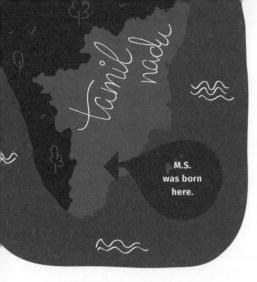

M.S. was born here.

her to sing 'Hari Tuma Haro', a devotional song by the mystic poet Mirabai. Following All India Radio's announcement of the Mahatma's death, Subbulakshmi's rendition of the song was played. Hearing her own voice, Subbulakshmi broke into tears.

Subbulakshmi went on to become a global phenomenon and travelled to many countries to perform. Her international break came with her performance at the Edinburgh International Festival of Arts. In 1966, the Secretary-General of the United Nations invited her to perform at a special concert at the UN Headquarters, making her the first Indian classical musician to have ever performed there. Thanks to her, the whole world discovered the glory and divinity of classical Indian music in its most pristine form.

M.S. Subbulakshmi has often been called the 'Goddess of the Perfect Note'. To India's top musicians, she is the 'Eighth Note of Music', superior even to the seven classical notes. Subbulakshmi was much more than a legendary musician; she was India's cultural ambassador in the pre-Independence era. Her soulful music enthralled audiences and transported listeners to worlds unknown. Speaking of her talent, Nehru famously said, 'Who am I, a mere Prime Minister before a Queen, a Queen of Music.'

Subbulakshmi also acted in a few Tamil films in her youth, most notably in *Meera*, which told the tale of Mirabai, the legendary mystic poet who first composed 'Hari Tuma Haro'. Playing Mirabai,

M.S. Subbulakshmi:
The Definitive Biography

1916 - 2004

she sang all the songs of the film. To nobody's surprise, the film became a major hit and was featured in international film festivals in Prague and Venice. Pandit Jawaharlal Nehru and the Mountbattens watched the film, and Sarojini Naidu christened M.S. with her own title 'The Nightingale of India'.

Until Subbulakshmi, Carnatic music was a male-dominated field. The Nightingale's voice paved the way for countless women to take part in the Carnatic arts and helped revive India's culture, at a time when it was fading against the oppression of colonial rule. Even the movies she starred in conveyed strong, patriotic messages. Subbulakshmi not only carved out a distinct place for women in the world of music and arts, but also played an important role in reviving the arts of the Devadasi community. As a philanthropist, she donated much of her earnings from concerts and royalties to support various records.

To this day, M.S. Subbulakshmi remains an icon for young female artists across the country.

Padma Bhushan Award (1954)

Padma Vibhushan Award (1975)

Indira Gandhi Award for National Integration (1990)

Bharat Ratna Award (1998)

Indian scholar of sanskrit

N for naheed abidi

won the Padma Sh

'Devalayasya dipah'

'sanskrit sahitya Mein Nahuni

{Naheed Abidi}

Only in India would you find a Muslim woman revered for being one of the foremost experts on Sanskrit, the language of the Hindu Vedas. One of the oldest of all human languages, Sanskrit is now spoken by less than one per cent of all Indians. Of its few speakers, only a handful are as skilled as Naheed Abidi, who has translated reams of Sanskrit poetry and holy texts into other languages.

*'Through my work on Rahim
I want to tell people that he (Rahim) had
great respect for Sanskrit and Hindu religion.'*

- Naheed Abidi

Suresh Chandra Banerji, in *A Companion to Sanskrit*, argued that despite often being misunderstood as a Hindu language, Sanskrit has had a long history of Islamic contributions. Building on this tradition, Naheed dedicated her life to Sanskrit, encouraging Muslims to study the language.

Naheed Abidi has a PhD in Sanskrit and is the first Muslim woman to have worked as a lecturer of the subject. She strongly believes in the language's potential to promote societal peace and harmony. Naheed has translated Urdu and Persian poetry into Sanskrit, as well as Sanskrit works into Hindi. In 2008, she translated Mirza Ghalib's *Charag-i-Dair* into a Sanskrit book called *Devalayasya Deepah*. In *Sanskrit Sahitya Mein*

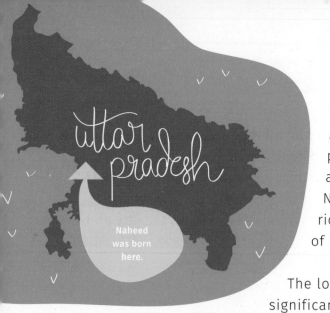

Rahim, she discusses the legendary poet Abdul Rahim Khan-e-Khana and his works. Through her works, Naheed opens up to the world a rich fusion of two different forms of beliefs.

The loss of Sanskrit has dealt a significant blow to the preservation of ancient Indian thought. India has a rich literary and religious Sanskrit heritage waiting to be revived, rediscovered and shared with the world. Sanskrit works, like the *Arthashastra*—a classic Vedic commentary on political economy and governance—rival better-known western works like Machiavelli's *Prince*. Ayurveda, one of the most ancient and effective practices of medicine and health, was initially recorded entirely in Sanskrit, though such works no longer survive in this language. Many Sanskrit scripts, such as the Sharda script that was once popular in Kashmir, and many Buddhist and Jain texts that were written in Sanskrit, are now completely lost.

books published by Naheed

Sanskrit Sahitya Mein Rahim

Devalayasya Deepa

Sirr-e-Akbar

Padma Shri Award (2014)

Like many other academic stalwarts, Naheed studies and researches her subject, while also balancing a family with two kids. But it was not easy for her to get paid for her work. Her first job as a lecturer teaching Sanskrit at the Banaras Hindu University was unpaid, and she followed this up by taking classes at the Mahatma Gandhi Kashi Vidyapith University for a very nominal salary.

Undeterred, and with a strong belief in the promise of the Sanskrit language, Naheed moved steadfastly ahead. She never let go of her passion, even at a time when all of India was transitioning towards Western cultural and linguistic influences. In recognition of her efforts in the field of literature, the Government of India presented Naheed with the Padma Shri Award in 2014. Upon receiving the award, Naheed said, 'Conferring Padma Shri Award upon me is like honouring the Sanskrit world, and it will inspire Muslims for Sanskrit learning.' Keeping alive a language and tradition that spans thousands of years, Naheed proves that India's legacy belongs to no single religion and is a shared torch for all to carry forward.

1961 – PRESENT

O for O.P. Ojaisha

Indian Olympic marathon runner

2 gold, 1 silver, 3 bronze

{ O.P. Jaisha }

Rising from the horrors of abject poverty, O.P. Jaisha is not the most successful or the most famous Indian athlete, but she certainly is one of the grittiest. Her journey—from having to eat mud for survival to becoming a national-level marathon record holder—is an awe-inspiring testimony to human resilience.

> *'When you have nothing to fall back on, you must grab the opportunity that comes your way and put your heart and soul into athletics. I did just that at Assumption College.'*
>
> **- O.P. Jaisha**

Born Orchatteri Puthiya Veetil Jaisha, O.P. Jaisha grew up in a tribal region within Kerala's lush Wayanad district. She knew poverty from an early age – her father worked as a daily-wage labourer in abject conditions. When she was just five years old, she saw him crippled by a tragic accident that left him bedridden forever. The incident forced them into extreme poverty, compelled to survive by eating mud. For a long time, just consuming rice water was a luxury for Jaisha and her family.

Despite everything, Jaisha still went to school. And one day, at a cultural festival, she was given a chance to run – as a last-minute replacement. Barefoot, Jaisha sprinted across the field and comfortably won the national school championship. Stunned by her strength and agility, the local coach put in a reference for her to acquire further

she ran and won her first race barefoot

training at Assumption College in Changanacherry, a breeding ground for athletes in Kerala.

From there started Jaisha's illustrious athletic career. She has represented India at several international events and brought home several medals. By the time she won her final medal, she was 32 years old – an age category that led many to think she was past her prime. But the very next year, she ran her first marathon and finished first, shattering the national-level women's marathon record, which had gone unchallenged for 19 years.

Throughout her life and career, Jaisha

O.P. Jaisha was born here.

Kerala

1983 – PRESENT

proved her naysayers wrong. She overcame poverty, injuries and all kinds of challenges. She turned every struggle into a victory. When her family could not provide for itself, Jaisha filled that role – a role traditionally seen as a man's job. She paid back all the loans her family had taken, got her sisters married and rebuilt her house.

If Jaisha's story tells us anything, it is that factors like gender, poverty or age cannot stop you when you are determined to pursue your passion.

Gold, First Asian Indoor Games, Bangkok (2005)

Silver, 1,500-metre, Asian Indoor Championships, Pattaya (2006)

Bronze, 3,000-metre, Asian Indoor Championships, Pattaya (2006)

Bronze, Commonwealth Games, Melbourne (2006)

Bronze, Doha Asiad (2006)

First Place, Indian Women Category, Mumbai Marathon (2015)

P.T. Usha

It's become a trope of sorts that when any young Indian girl shows signs of being a fast runner, she is dubbed 'P.T. Usha'. That's because, for much of the 1980s and 1990s, P.T. Usha was the fastest Indian woman, the country's greatest track and field athlete, and an icon for all Indian women athletes.

> *'In my opinion, happiness is nothing but satisfaction – satisfaction through work, thoughts and accomplishing our mission and vision.'*
>
> *- P.T. Usha*

Born in the village of Payyoli, in Kerala's Kozhikode district, Pilavullakandi Thekkeparambil Usha was used to falling sick. Much of her childhood was spent battling one illness or the other. She was not the kind of girl one would consider for athletics, and in the beginning, she was not to be seen on the sports field at all.

Yet, Usha loved to run and jump. She would often be seen sprinting barefoot on the beaches – and one of her favourite pastimes was leaping over fences. In the fourth grade, she was asked to run a race against the school champion, who was a few years her senior. She didn't expect to win. She just ran as fast as she could. But when she crossed the finish line, the school champion was behind her! This was the first time Usha realized her own talent. By the time she was in the

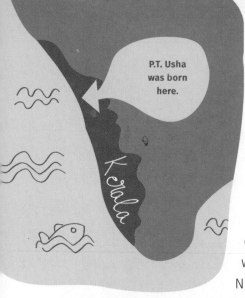

P.T. Usha was born here.

Kerala

seventh grade, she had become the district champion.

Usha has won numerous national and international track and field events in her career. She started her national career by winning the individual championship at the 1979 National Games in Delhi. She went on to become India's first and greatest hope for an Olympic medal in field sports. At Los Angeles, in 1984, she came closer to it than any other Indian before her, missing out on the bronze in the Olympic finals for 400-metre hurdles by a hundredth of a second. The very next year, she set several national records. Usha won five gold medals and one bronze at the Asian Track and Field Championships in Jakarta in 1985. In 1986, she claimed four golds and a silver at the Asian Games in Seoul and continued her spectacular run by winning three gold and two silver medals at the Asian Championships in Singapore in 1987.

Her unparalleled speed and perseverance earned her the nicknames 'Golden Girl' and 'Payyoli Express'. But with adoration came fierce criticism. When a heel injury prevented her from winning a medal at the 400-metre hurdles in the 1988 Seoul Olympics, her house was stoned, and she was accused of betraying the nation. Undeterred, she went on to win four gold and two silver medals at the 1989 Asian Athletics Championships.

Every time the world doubted Usha, she proved them wrong. She believed in herself, not in what others said about her – and this

Golden Girl:
The Autobiography of P.T. Usha

made all the difference. At the 1998 Asian Track Federation meet in Japan, Usha came home with a gold medal in the 4x100-metre relay, a silver

medal in the 4x400-metre relay and bronze medals in both the 200-metre and 400-metre events. A mother at the time, all her contemporaries had long since retired. But age did not stop Usha.

Having retired from active sports, Usha now uses her position in the athletic world to speak out against petty politics in sports, highlighting, in particular, the widespread discrimination meted out to women. Currently, she runs the Usha School of Athletics in Koyilandy near Kozhikode in Kerala, India, providing world-class facilities and helping train the athletes of tomorrow.

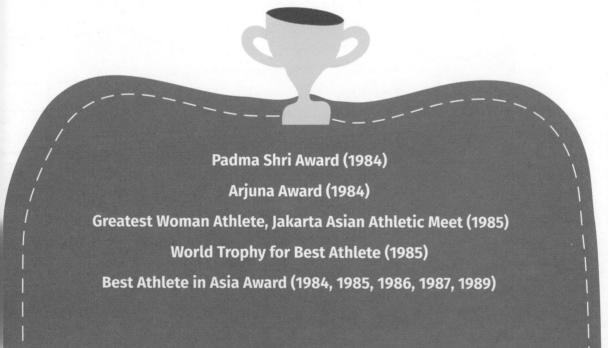

Padma Shri Award (1984)

Arjuna Award (1984)

Greatest Woman Athlete, Jakarta Asian Athletic Meet (1985)

World Trophy for Best Athlete (1985)

Best Athlete in Asia Award (1984, 1985, 1986, 1987, 1989)

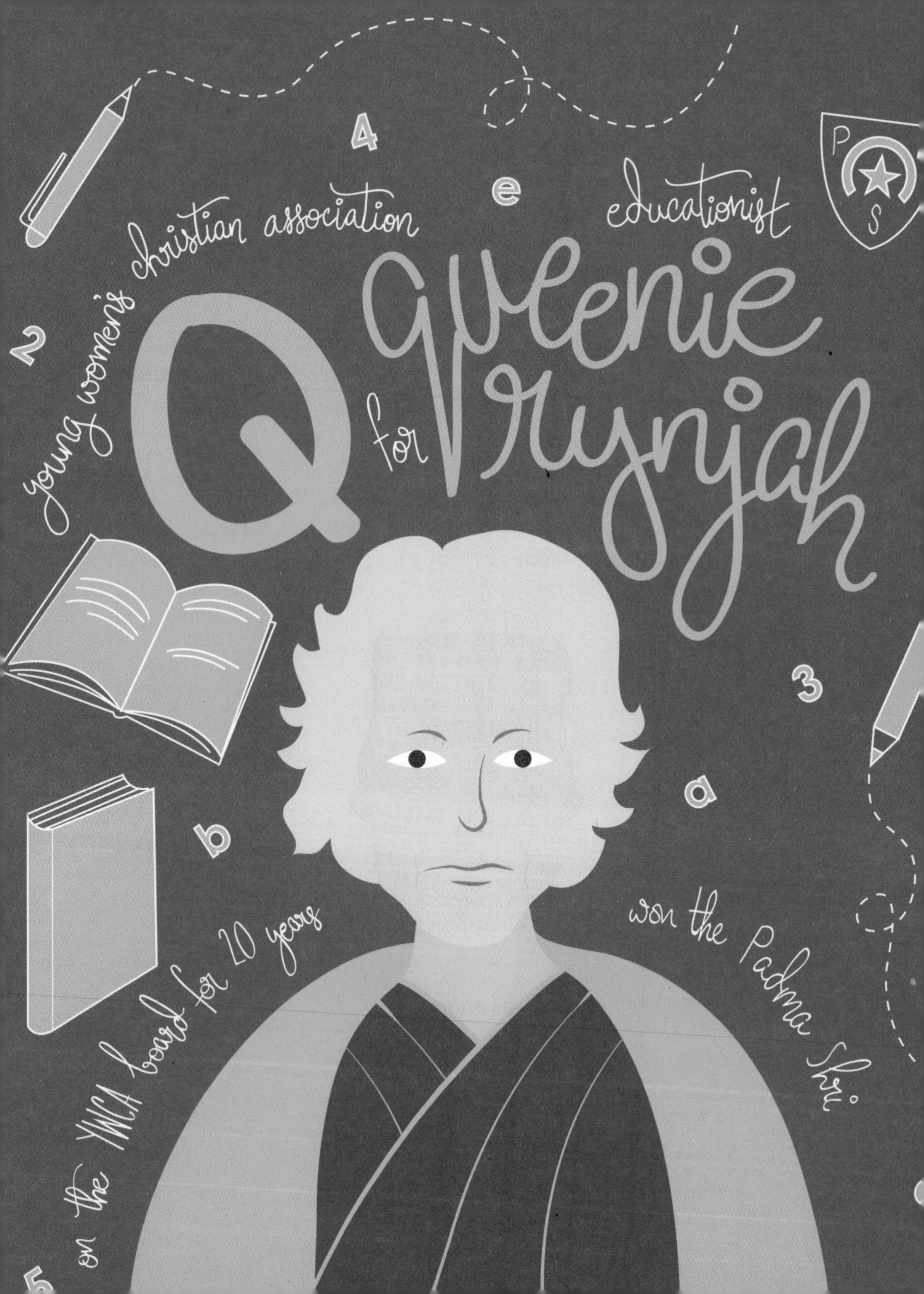

Q for Qvlenie Rynjah
young women's christian association
educationist
on the YWCA board for 20 years
won the Padma Shri
P S
4
e
2
3
a
b
5

Queenie Rynjah

Girl Scout, school principal, social worker – Queenie Rynjah exemplifies what it means to be a strong-willed woman. Her non-compromising approach to social work has made her one of Meghalaya's most renowned activists.

Queenie—born Queenie Madaline Dunn—displayed passionate leadership very early in her life. She received the 'Bluebird Guiders Warrant' by the Girl Guide Association of India in 1937 and later became one of the founding members of the Meghalaya Bharat Scouts and Guides. After her marriage, Queenie started teaching at the Pine Mount School in Shillong. She was a great teacher; her passion and hard work led to a successful 25-year-long career as headmistress of the Pine Mount School.

'To live a long life, keep[ing] a happy disposition is a gift.'

- Queenie Rynjah

When she retired from her career as an educationist, Queenie put all her energy into serving the community through her social work. Her passion for making a difference led to her success and wide acclaim. Queenie became the President of three of Shillong's key social organizations – the Ka Seng Teilang Kynthei, the Ka Synjuk Kynthei and the

Meghalaya

Queenie was born here.

Ka Lympung Ki Seng Kynthei. These organizations grew by leaps and bounds under Queenie's guidance as she helped unite them under a central leadership. The organizations benefited countless underprivileged residents by setting up vocational training centres that helped women become financially independent.

At Seng Teilang Ki Kynthei Laban, Queenie focused on empowering women. She founded the organization in 1979, during the peak of communal agitations in Meghalaya, when ordinary people suffered from frequent bandhs and shutdowns. Even long years of retirement didn't jade her sense of justice, and Queenie wrote an impassioned letter to the editor of the *Shillong Times* asking the protestors who burned public property to take constructive action. She wrote, 'Has this brought any benefit? Is this justified? No! Only loss, loss, loss. Insane destructive actions such as the burning of haystacks which are winter food for the animals! What will they eat the whole winter? What would you eat if your stock of food was burnt?'

Queenie actively worked in the areas of education and environment— with an emphasis on afforestation—and to eradicate violence against women. The

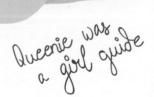

Queenie was a girl guide

Padma Shri Award (2004)

innovative and optimistic Queenie never allowed paucity of funds to limit her programmes. She held local fundraising events and sold goods to keep these initiatives alive. She helped train women in tailoring, knitting and embroidery, and led numerous drives to spread awareness about environmental conservation. She set up creches where young mothers could leave their children while they built their careers. Even when she was 90, she could be found making cloth balls from discarded clothes for the children that came to the creche.

A lifelong teaching career is itself quite fulfilling for those who desire to help others. However, Queenie continued to work for social causes beyond retirement and well into her old age. Queenie Rynjah is proof that gender, age or geographical limitations are no barriers for those who have the heart and the drive to work hard to make the world a better place.

1919 – 2015

Emmy award winner

journalist

R for

ruchira gupta

women's rights activist

Ruchira Gupta

The Selling of Innocents, an evocative and Emmy-Award-winning
documentary movie (under the News and Documentary category, 1997)
that looks at sex trafficking in India, was the brainchild of journalist
and activist Ruchira Gupta. Gupta is a policymaker, a sex-trafficking
abolitionist and a determined visionary who has testified to the Indian
Parliament on amending its trafficking laws. She is one of the loudest
voices and an indomitable force behind one of the world's biggest
organized movements fighting against prostitution, sex trade and
human trafficking.

> 'So, first they tried to make me hide it, then they tried to
> trivialize me, blame me, and when nothing would make me
> stop, they tried to marginalize me.'
>
> – Ruchira Gupta

Ruchira began her journey as a journalist with a keen interest in
highlighting women's rights. In her days as a journalist during the
demolition of the Babri Masjid in 1992, she herself faced sexual
harassment and public shaming. Earlier, while on an assignment in the
hills of Nepal, Ruchira noticed something strange about the village
she was passing by – there were no women in it. None at all. When she
asked why, the answer she got was horrifying: all of them had been

sold into the sex-trafficking industry in Mumbai. This became the subject of her documentary, *The Selling of Innocents*. The movie documents the flesh trade as it starts in Kathmandu and ends on Bombay's Falkland Road. The film inspired change across the world and even prompted the US Senate to pass the Trafficking Victims Protection Act.

Half the Sky:
Turning Oppression into Opportunity for Women Worldwide

But this accolade wasn't what Ruchira wanted; she had met too many women who had suffered in the flesh trade. She quit journalism to focus on activism and worked with 22 of the women featured in her documentary to found Apne Aap, a grassroots organization dedicated to ending sex trafficking.

Along with her team at Apne Aap, Gupta leads several women who were formerly part of the flesh trade to access education and acquire legal protection. Concerted efforts are made by Apne Aap to help rehabilitate these women in mainstream society. As a part of Gupta's activist career, she also produces the *Redlight Dispatch*, a newspaper written by and for the

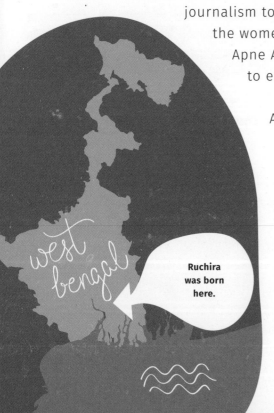

west bengal

Ruchira was born here.

1964 – PRESENT

victims and survivors of forced prostitution. She also takes classes at multiple universities, both in India and abroad, about the best practices in combating trafficking.

Fearless women like Ruchira, who are unbending in the face of opposition, work hard to make sure that the world becomes a better and safer place for everyone.

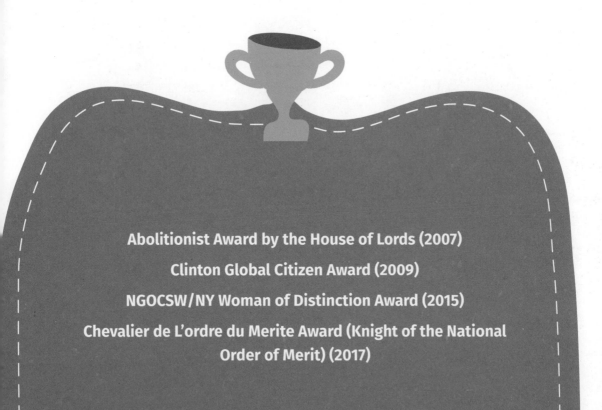

Abolitionist Award by the House of Lords (2007)

Clinton Global Citizen Award (2009)

NGOCSW/NY Woman of Distinction Award (2015)

Chevalier de L'ordre du Merite Award (Knight of the National Order of Merit) (2017)

Saina Nehwal

When Saina Nehwal was born, her grandmother was so upset that the child was a girl, she refused to meet her granddaughter for a whole month. Little did she know that this baby would one day be one of India's greatest badminton players. Today, with 16 international singles titles at the Super Series and Grand Prix Gold level, Saina—the darling daughter of India—ranks amongst the top badminton players of the world.

'If the future is tough, let it be. You have to fight tough situations. I have never played easy matches.'

– Saina Nehwal

Saina overcame many hurdles on her way to the top. Born in Hisar, Haryana, a region where people have deep-seated prejudices against girl children, Saina grew up with strict financial constraints. Her father held a government job and could barely provide for her sports-training expenses. However, Nehwal's parents never let her practice suffer, since they also had been badminton players and knew the importance of being able to exclusively focus on one's skill. They often borrowed money from friends and colleagues to keep supporting Saina. They helped her through her journey, waking up at 4 a.m. in the morning and taking her to the local stadium. Then, they would drop her at school. Even though she could barely make it in time for the morning assembly, Saina did her best to balance her schoolwork and her sporting career. She lived with razor-sharp discipline, her eyes set single-mindedly on winning an Olympic medal for India.

Saina Nehwal:
An Inspirational Biography

Playing to Win

Saina went on to become the first Indian sportsperson to win an Olympic medal in badminton. She is also the first to have won Commonwealth Gold in women's singles as well as the World Junior and Commonwealth Youth titles. The number one position in world badminton—once unachievable—came home when Saina became the first Indian woman to reach the top position in the Badminton World Federation global rankings.

Saina is a fighter—both on and off court—and has had to struggle at every point on her way to a win. Due to her strong playing style, she has sustained several injuries throughout her career. In 2014, when Saina suffered a terrible knee injury, her critics declared that her career was over, and she herself considered quitting badminton. However, the young athlete chose not to give up, and instead, made some important life changes. She switched training camps, worked hard on her fitness, and made sure that her body could cope with the fast-paced game. Her ability to focus and her mental strength helped her regain her confidence. As a result, in 2017, not

haryana

Saina
was born
here.

only was Saina still going strong, but she also won the Malaysia Masters Grand Prix, despite the career-threatening knee injury.

1990 – PRESENT

Today, Saina is one of the brand ambassadors for the 'Save The Girl Child' campaign in India, along with fellow Olympian Sakshi Malik, also from Haryana. Saina is amongst the most charitable sportspersons in the world; the only Indian on the 'Athletes Gone Good' list compiled by dosomething.org.

Saina's success brought a badminton boom in India, and several girls have now started taking up the sport, inspired by the powerful narrative that is Saina Nehwal's life.

Arjuna Award (2009)

Padma Shri Award (2010)

Rajiv Gandhi Khel Ratna (2009–10)

Padma Bhushan Award (2016)

T for tessy thomas
agni putri
$v = \sqrt{G \frac{M}{r}}$
won the Lal Bahadur Shastri award
missile woman of India
$\frac{v^2}{r} = g$
अग्नि-III
भारत

Tessy Thomas

If Dr A.P.J. Abdul Kalam is the Missile Man of India, then Tessy Thomas is the Missile Woman of the country. After all, it's her signature on the Agni series of intercontinental ballistic missiles – the backbone of India's nuclear deterrent. Tessy is not only the first woman to head a missile programme in India, but also one amongst a handful of women in the world to head a flagship missile programme of this magnitude. Considering the gender gap in the field of science in India, heading the nation's apex defence project has been a tremendous achievement for Tessy.

'A poster of Tessy in every Indian school will wreck stereotypes and create enormous career aspirations for girls.'

- Anand Mahindra
Chairman of the Mahindra Group

Tessy Thomas grew up near a rocket-launching station in Thumba, Kerala, which became the primary reason for her desire to become a rocket scientist. She launched her career by earning an M.Tech in Guided Missiles from the Defence Institute of Advanced Technology, Pune. She then went on to work at the Defence Research and Development Organization (DRDO), India's top military research establishment. There, Dr Abdul Kalam recognized her talent and handpicked her for the Agni missile programme.

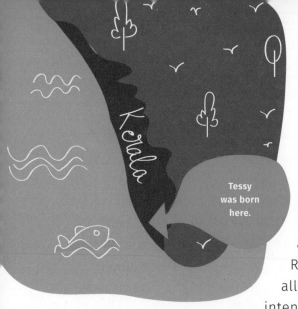

Kerala

Tessy was born here.

Within a few years of joining the Agni missile programme team, Dr Tessy Thomas designed a first-of-its-kind advanced missile guiding system for India. She also developed a revolutionary technology named RVS—Re-entry Vehicle System—that allows missiles to survive the heat-intensive process of re-entering the Earth's atmosphere. Tessy's role at Agni has been long and fruitful; she was the Associate Project Director of the 3,000-km range Agni-III, and then the Project Director for both Agni-IV and Agni-V ballistic missiles. With each project, she raised the profile of India's strategic capability.

Tessy is recognized and credited for making India self-reliant in the field of missile technology. In January 2012, the then Prime Minister Dr Manmohan Singh told the Indian

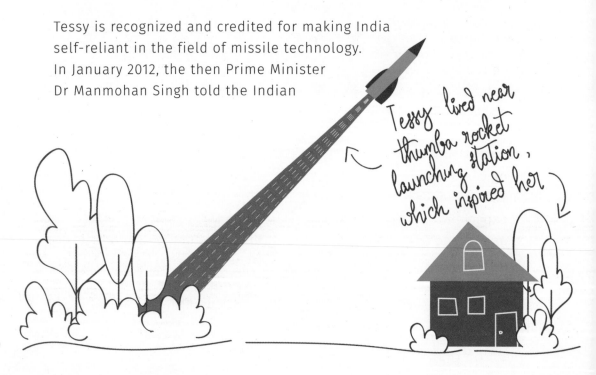

Tessy lived near thumba rocket launching station, which inspired her

Lal Bahadur Shastri National Award (2012)

Science Congress that Tessy is an example of a 'woman making her mark in a traditionally male bastion and decisively breaking the glass ceiling'.

It is unfortunate that many women feel that they are not cut out for a career in science. There is a societal bias that drives this mindset, causing many to think that women are unfit for certain professions. Fortunately, this is gradually changing. In the last 25 years, Tessy has seen an increasing number of female employees in her workplace.

If a woman sets her mind to a task, Tessy says, nothing can stop her from achieving it. There was a time when few would have expected a developing nation such as India to join the missile club. All it took was visionaries like Tessy, who looked beyond perceived limits and surpassed them with every opportunity.

1963 – PRESENT

Uma Devi Khatri

The word 'Tuntun', which is Uma Devi Khatri's nickname, is affectionately used as a synonym for a 'fat woman' in India. Interestingly, the word 'Tuntun' never faces any derogatory flak for its employment. This is because it reminds one of a very jovial, loving, innocent and strongly determined actor and comedienne: Uma Devi Khatri, the first female comedian of Hindi cinema.

> *'Don't for a moment think that I feel upset about people making fun of me or laughing at me. It reminds me in fact of my popularity.'*
>
> *– Uma Devi Khatri*

Uma was born to a conservative family and faced many hardships throughout her life. But she saw none of these as impediments. She lost her parents at the age of two and had to learn how to be strong for herself. When her uncle barred her from attending school, she taught herself to read and write. When she tried to break into an industry that saw her as being too fat or too dark to be a diva, she used her voice and sense of humour to get her foot in the door.

By the end of her life, with all her obstacles beaten, she was one of Bollywood's greatest singers, comedians and actresses.

Uma's innate talent and attraction towards film songs led her to come to Mumbai. To compensate for the lack of a formal training in music, Uma practised arduously. In order to get by in the big metropolis, she taught herself to read and write in Hindi, and learned how to speak a handful of English and Urdu words and phrases.

'babul' was her debut as an actress →

बाबुल

But even in Mumbai, this wasn't enough. If you've ever been to the great city, you'll know how intimidating it can feel to be surrounded by so many buildings and people – the richest and poorest in India alike. How does one make it in a city this big? For Uma, it was by marching boldly through the door of Bollywood's greatest composer at the time—Naushad Ali—and convincing him to give her a chance. This was how Uma got her break in Bollywood as a playback singer.

Uma was born here.

uttar pradesh

'Tuntun' was also smart about recognizing her own skills, appraising them for what they were and never failing to demonstrate and believe in them.

After a successful career as a playback singer, she went on to take up the challenge of becoming a comic actor. With her persistence and relentless pursuit to demand nothing but the best,

1923 - 2003

Uma Devi debuted opposite none other than the legendary actor, Dilip Kumar. From there on, she carved a niche for herself in comic roles in Bollywood and gained unprecedented popularity as a comedian. To this day, her mere presence in a movie can make the audience burst into laughter.

Comic roles in Bollywood are largely reserved for men and were especially so during Uma Devi's time. However, Uma Devi broke the glass ceiling for women in this space; her pursuit in realizing her dreams is an inspirational example of hard work, persistence and believing in oneself even when nobody else does.

A career spanning over 50 years, with nearly 200 films to her credit

{Vinita Bali}

In India's rapidly growing economy, consumer brands come and go, but there are few that sustainably stand the test of time and become an integral part of its contemporary culture. Rasna, the refreshing drink, and Britannia biscuits are two such iconic brands, and they both have Vinita Bali's name stamped upon them.

*'In fact, as I reflect on where and how
I have spent my time in the corporate world,
the overarching theme is one of going with the flow
and pursuing a path that was interesting and different,
rather than conventional.'*

– Vinita Bali

The first woman to head a consumer brand company in India, Vinita paved the way for consumer goods to enter developing markets across the world. She stands tall amongst a short list of extremely successful Indian brand marketers and businesswomen. Through her steely grit and hard work, she powered her way to the top of the business echelon, both in India and globally. Nestle, Coca-Cola, Britannia and Titan – her resume is essentially a list of the world's top corporations.

Vinita's first professional stint was at Voltas (through Tata), after she finished her MBA. At Voltas, she re-launched Rasna, turning it into a raging success

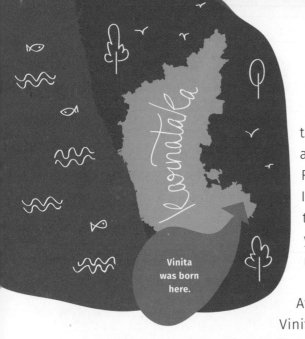

Vinita was born here.

Karnataka

that became the defining drink of the 80s and 90s. Inspired by Vinita's success with Rasna, Cadbury hired her to boost its India operations, where she then helped triple sales in three years. Over the years, several multinational companies reached out to her for her expertise.

After working with Coca-Cola in Chile, Vinita headed back home to help revive an Indian food company—Britannia—that was struggling at the time. She was appointed its CEO in 2005, and with that, Vinita became the first woman to head a publicly listed food company in India. Under her leadership, Britannia made its biscuits healthier and re-emerged as a strong Indian brand. They even supplied biscuits to the World Food Programme, which inspired Vinita to launch the iron-fortified 'Tiger' brand of biscuits in India. With this, Vinita aimed to tackle India's nutrition crisis.

Despite working in several major companies in several countries, Vinita never felt she encountered a glass ceiling – simply because her work always spoke for her. She had a knack for making pleasant opportunities come her way. When Cadbury posted her in Bourneville, United Kingdom, she used the town's proximity to Stratford-Upon-Avon (Shakespeare's birthplace) to watch every single one of the Bard's plays. When she wanted a sabbatical, she took up the chance to pursue a one-year scholarship at Michigan State University. Her willingness to work anywhere saw

Living Legends, Learning Lessons:
Up, Close And Personal With 10 Global Icons

Vinita has lived and worked in 6 countries across 5 continents.

her travel the world, running and reviving big businesses on multiple continents. She was the first woman ever to hold a position on the board of Cadbury Nigeria and South Africa.

Vinita Bali had some unique management credos, one of which was to invite artists to speak to her team about how businesses could draw from the arts and from creative practice. A student of Kathakali for 16 years, she knew how the arts could help train one's mind to focus well.

After quitting the consumer goods industry, Vinita took up the cause of child malnutrition, heading the Britannia Nutrition Foundation (BNF). She has also spent many years working with the Geneva-based Global Alliance for Improved Nutrition (GAIN).

According to Vinita, to be really good at what you do requires an immense amount of hard work and determination, an ability to take risks, and the determination to not allow biases to dissuade you from taking up challenges.

1955 – PRESENT

W for wahida prism khan

INS Arroa (A54)

first kashmiri female officer of the Indian Navy

first woman to command the AFMC parade

Wahida Prism Khan

When Wahida joined the Indian Navy in 1997, it had only been five years since women were first allowed in combat roles in the naval branch of the armed forces. Growing up in Jammu and Kashmir, she had never seen a woman army officer, but she never let these factors deter her. Today, as Surgeon Lt. Commander, she is the first woman from the militancy-marred state to serve in the Indian Navy.

'Nothing is impossible if you are determined. Parents should give total freedom to their daughters in matters of career choice and daughters should live up to that trust.'

- Wahida Prism Khan

Right from her childhood, Wahida was fascinated and intrigued by the Indian Armed Forces. Although she never saw a woman army officer, Wahida never got discouraged or assumed that an army career was only for men. She always dreamt of joining the armed forces one day. Throughout her schooling, Wahida was an active student leader, commanding platoons at the school, college and state level. Wahida's father, Gulzar Ahmed, the headmaster of a government school, was also a huge influence on her. He taught his children to work hard and inculcated a strong work ethic in them. While most people in their village were extremely conservative in their outlook towards women,

Jammu & Kashmir

Wahida was born here.

Gulzar Ahmed wanted his daughters to be fearless and independent. Inspired by the prism's seven reflecting colours, her father gave Wahida her middle name – Prism.

After completing her medical education from Jammu, Wahida could have easily started her private practice, but the call of the Naval forces was more appealing to her. In November 1997, after completing her training courses, Wahida was commissioned into the Navy – a first for a woman from J&K. She served aboard the INS Amba for 19 months.

In 2006, Wahida became the first woman to command the Armed Forces Medical College (AFMC) parade, a highly prestigious honour in the Indian Armed Forces.

Just like in other aspects of her life, Wahida was bold in choosing her life partner as well. She married Major M.F. Khan, a pathologist and

Wahida's father inspired by the 7 reflecting colours, named her 'Prism'

former short-service commissioned Indian Army Officer, who was junior to her in service. Marrying below one's rank is a practice still considered taboo in Indian society. 'Though he was junior to me in service, I knew he would understand my commitment to work and all odds and evens associated with it,' Wahida is reported to have said.

In 2007, the National Council of Education Research and Training (NCERT) incorporated her unique story in a chapter of a Class IV textbook, to inspire students—particularly young girls—across the country to unhesitatingly reach for the stars. Wahida's relentless drive and her courage to follow her heart shows that gender hurdles can be overcome if you are determined to achieve your goals.

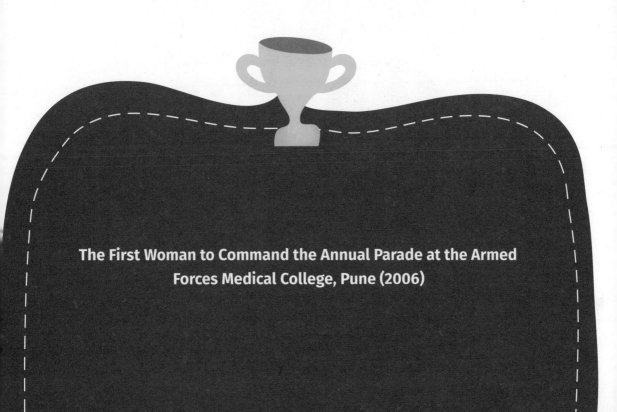

The First Woman to Command the Annual Parade at the Armed Forces Medical College, Pune (2006)

{ Xtraordinary }

X is for all the readers of this book who are extraordinary in their own special and unique way. Each one of you is a role model to someone in this world. We are constantly struggling and smashing several glass ceilings; thus, it is only natural that our path is closely followed and our moves closely observed. Therefore, we do not get to decide whether we want to be a role model or not, we just get to choose what kind of a role model we want to be. So choose right and choose well, dear reader/fighter/survivor – all!

'Being a woman means I am a role model – like it or not.'

- Jane Clarke
Professor of Molecular Biophysics

X is also for all the extraordinary women of the past, present and future who have fought, and will fight, for themselves and for those they love. X is for all the women who run businesses and boost our economies, and for women who nurture our houses and make them homes. It is for the women who fight diseases, disabilities and setbacks with courage and grit. X is for those women who fight for their own dignity and for ours, for their own rights and ours, and who strongly believe in women's rightful place under the sun. X is also for

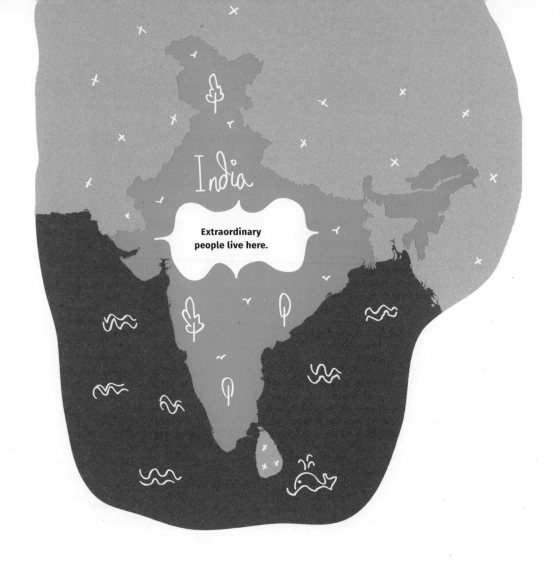

India

Extraordinary
people live here.

all the boys who don't just think of girls as prizes to be won, but as
doers and thinkers worthy of respect.

While this book documents women who were successful in various
professional fields, it is important to note that being extraordinary
is not defined only by one's successful career. Living and leading a
life of integrity and authenticity is more a mark of success than one's
professional feats. No profession is good or bad, and these stories are
only meant to showcase how women's potential must not be limited

in terms of what the world thinks they can or cannot do. Do not let society stand in the way of your dreams, because the key to being truly extraordinary is to have a goal and a firm belief that it can be achieved in the face of all odds. Your gender or your physical appearance should not decide where life takes you. One should always remember that it is compassion, perseverance, grit, pragmatism, determination and conviction in one's personal capacities that will lead to a successful future.

Will Durant, in his book *The Story of Philosophy*, said, 'We are what we repeatedly do. Excellence, then, is not an act, but a habit.' So, here's our hope for you: make excellence a habit, pursue your dreams, fight for your rights, and spread your light wherever you go. Strong role models light their own candles and ignite others along the way.

Y for **yamini krishnamurthy**

bharatnatyam & kuchipudi dancer

awarded the padma vibhushan

शुक्र

हंसास्य

अलपद्म

Yamini Krishnamurthy

With her flashing arms, thrumming feet, an evocative body and enthralling eyes, Yamini Krishnamurthy's presence on stage makes people gasp in awe and wonder. Her vivacious eyes and ever-humming lips—bursting with emotions and life—always had a hold on everyone's heart. Indeed, Yamini's dynamism and charisma on stage has gripped her audience's attention for several decades. It is no surprise then that people call Yamini Krishnamurthy the 'actual diva of dance' and 'poetry in motion.'

> *'A dance performance is rather like going out into a battlefield. You have to hold the attention of as many as five to 10,000 people, a lot of whom do not follow your language.'*
>
> *- Yamini Krishnamurthy*

By the age of five, Yamini knew that she wanted to become a professional dancer. The revelation came to her as she trailed behind her mother at the Chidambaram temple in Tamil Nadu. The temple—dedicated to Nataraj, the God of Dance—features 108 beautifully carved sculptures depicting each dance transition featured in the Natya Shastras. Staring at these figurines, Yamini would feel an urge to dance. By the age of 28, she had danced her way to the Padma Shri, awarded to her by the then Prime Minister Jawaharlal Nehru.

A Passion for Dance

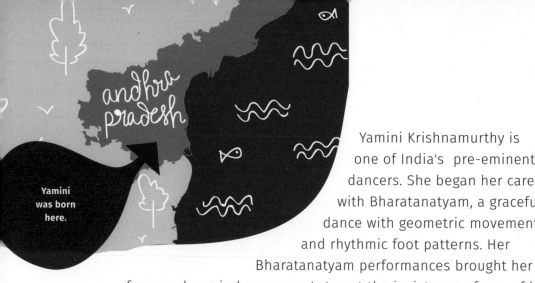

andhra pradesh

Yamini was born here.

Yamini Krishnamurthy is one of India's pre-eminent dancers. She began her career with Bharatanatyam, a graceful dance with geometric movements and rhythmic foot patterns. Her Bharatanatyam performances brought her fame early on in her career. Later, at the insistence of one of her teachers, she learnt Kuchipudi, a quicker and more spontaneous dance, which, at that time, was still considered a folkdance form and not a classical one.

She later became the torchbearer of Kuchipudi, well into the twilight years of her performing career. Yamini also started learning Odissi when its leading gurus were still codifying the dance form. She trained with two of them – Guru Pankaj Charan Das and Kelucharan Mohapatra and became one of its leading performers. Soon, she could easily perform three different classical dance forms with equal flair and skill. Yamini is therefore aptly referred to as the doyenne of Bharatanatyam, Kuchipudi, and Odissi – three out of eight recognized classical dance forms in India.

the Karnas on the Nataraja temple inspired Yamini ↓

Yamini toured all over India, performing in various Andhra Mahasabhas and Telugu associations. She was the first person to perform Kuchipudi in London, at a Commonwealth conference. She has also performed across Europe, Russia and America.

Yamini is also trained in Carnatic vocal music and can play the veena, a stringed instrument. Her dance studio, the Yamini School of Dance, was launched in Delhi in 1990 and imparts intensive classical dance training to young and aspiring dancers. She created a 13-part dance programme for the Doordarshan TV channel. Her book, *A Passion for Dance*, was unanimously recommended by critics.

Yamini Krishnamurthy's career is a dazzling display of our country's rich traditions and culture. Her performances have brought international recognition to classical Indian folk dances, carrying forward centuries worth of India's dance heritage. Yamini is a trendsetter and role model for several generations of dancers and aspiring performers, and her devotion towards dancing has given the world decades of inspiration to draw from.

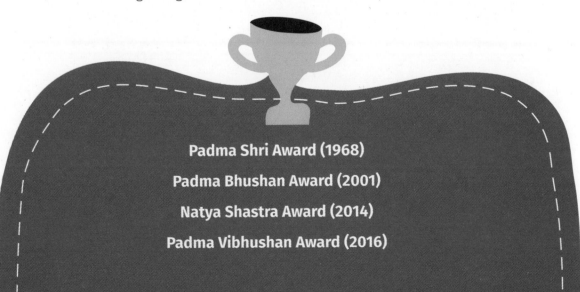

Padma Shri Award (1968)

Padma Bhushan Award (2001)

Natya Shastra Award (2014)

Padma Vibhushan Award (2016)

Zohra Sehgal

Zohra Sehgal—actor, dancer, choreographer—is one of those rare centenarians who managed to preserve her childhood in the form of boundless energy that never waned with age. She was one of India's famous jaunty personalities who augmented her looks with her signature cheerfulness and the positivity of her mind and spirit. Indeed, she was one of India's beloved actresses and dancers and will always be remembered for her sunny smile, her playful eyes and her impeccable acting. At school, Zohra took part in plays and shone on stage from the very beginning.

'You see me now when I am old and ugly, in fact you should have seen me earlier — when I was young and ugly!'

– Zohra Sehgal

Her boisterous tomboy nature notwithstanding, when it was time for Zohra to get married, she wrote to her uncle, stating firmly that she did not want to get married! To her surprise, he replied saying that she was free to do anything she liked. This in a time when girls were expected to be married off by the time they turned 15.

But what would she do? Ideas were tossed around.

Her brother asked her if she wanted to become India's first female pilot. Zohra was game for it but did not want her father to worry about her safety. In turn, her father suggested that she take up theatre in England.

U.S.a

egypt

japan

And so, Zohra travelled by land across Asia to Europe, with her uncle who lived in Edinburgh.

Zohra always embraced life with ambition and determination. In her long and expansive career, she acted in Bollywood and Hollywood movies and in theatres; danced, choreographed and sang on stage; and taught in classrooms. She was the first Indian woman to learn a contemporary dance like the ballet in Germany and joined the troupe of India's legendary dancer and choreographer, Uday Shankar. With this troupe, she performed in Japan, Egypt, Europe and the United States.

Zohra's personality made her a natural star. She worked until the age of 100 and did so with untiring energy and acting prowess. Her short yet impressive roles in Hindi cinema made her one of the most famous and most hilarious 'Bollywood grannies'.

Zohra was born here.

uttar pradesh

1912 – 2014

Apart from acting in several films in India and abroad, Zohra also gained massive popularity through her poetry recitals. She received immense adoration for her profound and evocative rendition of Hafeez Jullundhri's famous nazm, 'Abhi To Main Jawan Hoon'.

Zohra overcame all obstacles and hardships that life threw her way. She could not see with one eye from her infancy due to glaucoma and was diagnosed with cancer later in 1994. However, her willpower and vivacity helped her tide over these difficulties. In her own words, 'Life's been tough, but I've been tougher. I beat life at its own game.'

Zohra was the embodiment of a woman who was always high-spirited and unbelievably confident. Her positive approach to life drove her career to every imaginable height. It wasn't all fun and games – she had to work hard and long to get where she did. But, through it all, she proved that she could do everything she wanted to do. When the end came, she accepted it gracefully, knowing that she had fought the good fight for a century and more!

Zohra is an example of drawing contentment from life and serves as an inspiration to keep smiling and striving through all hardships.

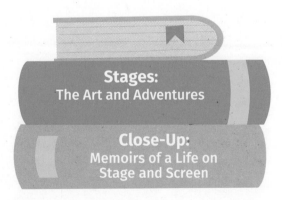

Stages:
The Art and Adventures

Close-Up:
Memoirs of a Life on
Stage and Screen

The She Can
You Can Contest

In the run up to the making of this book, we ran a contest inviting children to tell us about how they have been role models to someone else in their lives. Here are the two entries that best embody the essence of this book – that if SHE can, YOU can.

The Joy of Giving

by Avigna N.S.
(Class VII, Chennai)

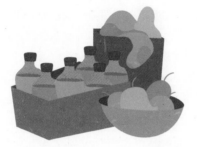

In 2015, Chennai had one of the darkest phases in its history. The city was completely flooded, and its people were stranded. As people shared their stories of suffering, I got an idea. I gathered all the kids from the complex and came up with a plan. I led a door-to-door campaign to persuade people to donate as much as they could. By evening, we had collected a huge pile of stuff. With the help of adults, we transported and donated these things to the people in need in the nearby localities. This was one of the greatest moments in my life so far, as I inspired not only myself but also the other children and adults around me.

My 'Real' Coach

by Shrishti Sharma
(Class IX, Nagpur)

When my debut attempt to set the Guinness World Record for the Lowest Limbo Skating on Ice failed, my father ordered a special pair of Double Blade Ice Skates designed by Bob Skates from Canada. To our dismay, the blades were too thin and suffered damage on the ice. My father then decided to make me a pair himself. He suffered several injuries during this task, including a severe injury to the third finger of his foot when a hand-cutter slipped and fell from his hands. At the age of 13, I attempted to set the same record once more wearing the customized skates painstakingly made by my father. I set a Guinness World Record for the Lowest Limbo Ice Skating over 10 metres and made my family and my country very proud. The experience taught me that when commitment, dedication, perseverance and unconditional love come together, nothing is impossible.

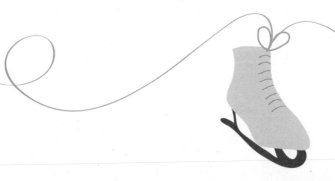

Activity 1
Craft a Line
Cut out the bookmark and the post card below
along the dotted lines.

Craft a Line Continued

Scribble a message, write a note, send it to a loved one
or keep it for yourself as a motivator. Spread the inspiration.

SHE can
you CAN

If she could do it,
You and I can do it too!
— Garima & Anastasia

SHE can
you CAN

If she could do it, You and I can do it too!
— Garima & Anastasia

Role-Model Search

Look up women in the following professions and write
their names in the space provided below.

Amrita Sher-Gil

Eulie Chowdhury

Nita Mehta

Kiran Bedi

Disha Oberoi

Harshini Kanhekar

Write a Biography

Use the spaces below to write a biography about your
role model or your future self.

_____

(name)

Introduction

_____
_____
_____
_____

Write a quote about or by your role model.

Early Life

_____
_____
_____

Career

_____

_____

_____

_____

Mention or draw a fun fact about yourself or your role model. ↗

Achievements

_____

_____ to _____
birth year   present year or year of death

Conclusion

_____

_____

_____

_____

_____

_____

Awards

Write down the awards you'd like to win
or awards your role model has won.

_____

_____

_____

supporters

This book would not have been possible without the generous contributions, love and support of all these people:

A for
Abhishek Chaturvedi
Achal Kathuria
Aditi Gupta
Alex Neylan
Alok Juneja
Angie Rai

B for
Bhawna Bhandari

C for
Christine Geeng

D for
Diwakar Kaushik

G for
Giridhar Hariharan
Govind Kaushal
Gyan Srivastava

H for
Harleen Parmar
Harsha Hardhagari
Himanshu Kapoor

I for
Ian Arawjo

L for
Lav Nigam
Lavanya Shanbhogue Arvind

M for Madhu Prakash

N for
Nandita Jayaraj
Nishant Singh
Neha Karajgikar
Noel Sequeira

P for
Palashi Vaghela
Paridhi Jaisingh
Parul Gandhi
Pooja Mittal
Pooja Patel
Prashant Prabhu
Pooja Rajanna
Pooja Sharma

R for
Radhika Bhandari Jassal
Radhika Chandramohanr
Radhika Goel
Rahul Thathoo
Ravi Kushwaha
Richa Gupta
Rohini Pandhi
Roli Agrawal
Ruchie Kothari

S for
Sanchita Gargya
Sandeep Kalidindi
Sanjeev Dhavala
Sanyam Bhasin
Sayali Kushwaha
Shachi Katira
Sherali Tukra
Shreya Bagthariya
Shruti Agarwal
Siddharth Venkatesh
Sireesha Katragadda
Sneha Narayanan
Srijan Kaushik
Sugandha Bhandari

T for
Tanush Parihar
Tuhin Paul

U for
Uday Kiran Medisetty
Upma Gupta

V for
Vasudhara Kantroo

Y for
Yair Levinson

The Bookmakers

Author

Garima is a scientist with a PhD in Bioinformatics. She has written for platforms like Menstrupedia, Youth Ki Awaaz and Women's Web on issues centered on women empowerment.

With this book, she hopes to inspire young girls to realize that there is no set profession for girls, and they can become whatever they aspire to be.

Garima

Co-Author

Rajat is the editor and production manager for *Menstrupedia*, an educational comic book and web platform that addresses menstrual myths and taboos.

With this book, Rajat wants young boys to unlearn the idea of girls as prizes to be won, and see them as doers and thinkers worthy of respect.

rajat

Illustrator

Anastasia is an illustrator, designer and musician. She illustrates children's books, ed-tech products and creates innovative music curriculum for children. Anastasia has worked with Stones2milestones, Chinmaya Mission and Kobus Neethling.

With this book, Anastasia strives to reinforce the fact that a person is more than just their appearance or gender.

anastasia